ETHNICITY AND PUBLIC POLICY

WINSTON A. VAN HORNE
EDITOR

THOMAS V. TONNESEN
MANAGING EDITOR

UNIVERSITY OF WISCONSIN SYSTEM
AMERICAN ETHNIC STUDIES COORDINATING
COMMITTEE / URBAN CORRIDOR CONSORTIUM

VOLUME I

ETHNICITY AND PUBLIC POLICY SERIES

University of Wisconsin System American Ethnic Studies
Coordinating Committee / Urban Corridor Consortium
P. O. Box 413, Milwaukee, WI 53201

International Standard Book Number ISBN 0-942672-00-3 (cloth)
International Standard Book Number ISBN 0-942672-01-1 (paper)
Library of Congress Catalog Card Number: 81-71991

CONTENTS

UNIVERSITY OF WISCONSIN SYSTEM AMERICAN ETHNIC STUDIES COORDINATING COMMITTEE

DR. WINSTON A. VAN HORNE
>University of Wisconsin–Milwaukee
>Chairperson, AESCC

DR. PETER J. KELLOGG
>University of Wisconsin–Green Bay

DR. LIONEL A. MALDONADO
>University of Wisconsin–Parkside

DR. WILLIAM J. MURIN
>Director, Urban Corridor Consortium

DR. MELVIN C. TERRELL
>University of Wisconsin–Oshkosh

MR. THOMAS V. TONNESEN
>Program Coordinator, AESCC (ex officio)

The University of Wisconsin System American Ethnic Studies Coordinating Committee (AESCC) wishes to acknowledge the contributions of its former members, as well as those of the Urban Corridor Consortium Steering Committee and the University of Wisconsin System American Ethnic Studies Advisory Committee.

Introduction

Winston A. Van Horne

University of Wisconsin-Milwaukee

The launching of any new venture is risky business. A movie producer does not know empirically, despite his best efforts grounded in long years of experience, whether the film he is about to release will be a smashing success or a dismal failure at the box office. Generally speaking, advertising does not make a movie a financial success; it is word of mouth that does the trick. So it is with a new academic publication. It is the word of mouth, oral and written, of ones' peers, as well as of other interested persons who contemplate and make use of the simple and complex ideas with which it is concerned, that determines a volume's success or failure.

This volume is the first in a series that will emanate from the University of Wisconsin System American Ethnic Studies Coordinating Committee's annual Green Bay Colloquium on "Ethnicity and Public Policy." Its purpose is to discuss rigorously the logical, conceptual and empirical elements of ethnicity and public policy.

Ethnicity entails the complex of biological attributes and social behaviors that give form and content to a distinguishable and separable clustering of human beings. Public policy entails the methods and techniques used by officials to formulate and implement authoritative decisions binding upon all, even though they affect individuals and groups differently. In a multiracial and multiethnic society such as ours, in which interests and purposes often differ sharply within and between racial and ethnic groups, what precisely *is, can,* and *ought to be* the role of public policy in the actualization of the common good? And what is the relation between that common good and the particular interests of given racial and ethnic groups?

Underlying these questions is the age-old philosophic problem of the relation between the universal and the particular; but there is more than just a puzzle for philosophers engaged in recondite reasoning involved here, given the societal significance of the empirical fact that today eighty-three different languages are spoken in Los Angeles, the second largest city in the country. The diversity of languages spoken there is a poignant representation of the burgeoning ethnic differentiation of our society. This alarms some, agitates others, and vexes still others who worry about (1) the capacity of the society to satisfy their own particular interests and purposes; (2) the spread of what may be called the Babel Curse, the inability and/or unwillingness of groups and individuals to see the actualization of their particular interests and purposes in the realization of the common good; (3) the loss of national cultural coherence; and (4) the danger of societal overload from excessive competing, conflicting, and/or contradictory demands upon the political system.

There are, however, those who perceive the continued and expanded ethnic cross-fertilization of our society as not only a source of cultural renewal and enrichment, but also as a social antibiotic to national chauvinism and ethnocentrism fostering the sort of smug complacency of which Alexander Solzhenitsyn has complained loudly and bitterly in his recent chastisement of the West in general, and America in particular. From this vantage point ethnic diversity is rather to be encouraged, for it secretes into the societal bloodstream defenses against the sort of social and cultural homogeneity that skews a people's sense of balance and proportion, making them haughty, conceited, insular, and self-righteous. These two dispositions energize many discussions, decisions, and actions pertaining to ethnicity and public policy.

The issue of the receptivity and responsiveness of American public policy to expanding ethnic diversity is joined in the following pages by Ronald Takaki and Nathan Glazer through the concepts of societal exclusiveness and inclusiveness. Both men agree that American society is marked by an inclusive-exclusive tradition of public policy which structures the life chances of racial and ethnic groups. But they disagree sharply—one might even say radically—over the defining attributes of the tradition, as well as its present effects on our society. Put starkly, Takaki believes that American public policy is grounded in a tradition of intensive white ethnic inclusion and extensive racial exclusion. Glazer, on the other hand, believes that the public policy of the American polity is noteworthy for the sustained expansion of ideas and actions designed to include diverse ethnic and racial groups into the web of social relations that give meaning and purpose to the social order, and also designed to continue contracting ideas and actions that exclude individuals and groups from full participation in the political community. Takaki and Glazer thus represent fundamentally differ-

vi

ent approaches to the problems accompanying ethnicity, race, and public policy in our society.

Takaki's belief is grounded in the very basic distinction he draws between a racial pattern and an ethnic pattern. The former entails a structure of social relations in which racial considerations are the primary determinants of individual and collective behaviors. An ethnic pattern entails an order of social relationships in which elements of ethnicity are the primary determinants of conduct towards an individual or group possessing a specified range of attributes. Takaki believes that America, from its founding to the present, is marked by a strong exclusionary impulse towards non-whites. He draws upon the views of Benjamin Franklin and Thomas Jefferson to corroborate the claim that America's non-white exclusivist and white inclusivist tradition is grounded in the ideas of the men who founded the Republic.

Unlike Takaki, Glazer does not draw a sharp distinction between a racial pattern and an ethnic pattern. He sees the race/ethnic distinction as one of a continuum from the worst treated to the best treated groups. With the race/ethnic question placed on a continuum, Glazer observes a continuous process of group declustering at the continuum's worst treated end and group reclustering towards its best treated end. This dynamic process confutes the static quality that Takaki perceives in race/ethnic relations in America.

Glazer believes that Takaki exaggerates unduly the uniformity of the role of race in America, especially in the latter part of the nineteenth century, and fails to come to grips with the significance of the continuous evolution of the society "towards a better state," grounded in the ideal of a color-blind society, which ascribes ultimate value to the individual. All good societal arrangements recognize, nurture, and protect the dignity, worth, value and inviolability of the individual qua individual. Glazer perceives this in America's inclusivist tradition, which has impelled it to embrace people from the world over.

Scrutinizing America's history in relation to race and ethnicity, Glazer observes three distinct periods. The first, from the founding of the Republic to the end of the Civil War, is marked by the racially exclusivist tradition that Takaki makes the touchstone of the history of race and ethnicity in America. It is, of course, noted for its regressive and oppressive formal/legal social structures, relations, and proscriptions. The second, from the end of the Civil War to the mid-1960s, is known for the "cloak of ignorance" that shielded the individual from considerations pertaining to race and/or ethnicity in so far as these could either advantage or disadvantage one unduly. This fostered a significant increase in the number of individuals at the better treated end of the continuum mentioned earlier. The ideal of the color-blind society fused with the cloak of ignorance to produce practices that ennobled the individual and enriched the society as the inclusivist tradition superceded the exclusivist one of the earlier period.

Period three, from the mid-1960s to the present, is marked by the decline of the ideal of the color-blind society and the rise of a new color consciousness ripping away the cloak of ignorance that previously shielded the individual. If the individual qua individual was preeminent in the second period, Glazer sees the group qua group as preeminent in the third. As the cloak of ignorance has been removed, the individual has sought refuge in the group—racial and ethnic considerations are now of critical importance in the distribution of society's benefits and burdens. Today the individual secures inclusion through the group, where previously it was secured on one's own.

Glazer's periodization is extremely sensitive to America's inclusivist impulses. Takaki believes that this is unfortunate, for it skews Glazer's perception of the measure of racial inclusion in the structural and institutional arrangements of the political community in periods two and three. He does not deny that since the end of the Civil War, inclusion of racial and non-white ethnic minorities into the extant interests and purposes of the political community has increased noticeably. He believes this inclusion, however, has evolved within a basically exclusionary framework. It is Takaki's conviction that the structures and institutions that sustain the exclusivist tradition reproduce themselves through several cross-sections of historical time and foster discrimination not always accompanied by overt and intentionally discriminatory actions. The inclusion of individuals and groups of racial and non-white ethnic minorities has been noticeable but unspectacular, given their nominal roles in the making and implementing of key public policy decisions, or of private decisions with major public policy significance.

There has been a measure of inclusion of these minorities into the political community, but at what cost, Takaki asks. He maintains inclusion is simultaneously a process of becoming and a state of being. As a process of becoming, it renews and increases the membership of the political community; as a state of being, it is a partnership in the ideas and actions that bind together and nurture the members of the political community, giving them their distinctiveness as a people. It is thus a compound of at least five distinct but nonetheless related elements. These are: (1) an ontological-epistemological-ethical triad that grounds its structure of ideas; (2) a set of formal/legal rules that order conduct sanctioned publicly; (3) a set of informal rules that order conduct which carries no public sanction; (4) forms of political and economic participation; and (5) a sense of belonging to, and feeling a part of, the political community. Takaki believes that when one reflects on Glazer's continuum, one discerns a "hard dark line" which is racial. This line extracts a high cost of inclusion from racial and non-white ethnic minorities.

The cost is observed in the surrender or camouflage of cultural norms, the ceaseless struggle for social acceptance, the persistent doubts pertaining to the affirmation and actualization of the self, and the marginality of participation in the society's political economy. Still, Takaki acknowledges there are benefits, for inclusion is accompanied by a range of privileges and entitlements that increase significantly the life chances of individuals and groups. This point is of telling importance for Glazer, who believes that Takaki exaggerates unduly the cost of inclusion.

Glazer observes that the cost of inclusion is usually borne *voluntarily*. Racial and ethnic minorities are neither compelled nor coerced to be included in the political community. Most desire and strive to be included. However, there are groups that have consciously sought radical exclusion, for example the Amish. Glazer believes inclusion does not entail total cultural homogenization or assimilation; it is quite amenable to cultural diversity and pluralism. The crucial point here is that there is a measure of shared interests and purposes for the good of all in (1)-(5) above that constitutes the minimal content of inclusion, the realization of which invariably carries a cost. Is this cost unfair to racial and non-white ethnic minorities? Glazer is unwilling to answer "no" unequivocally, for he is quite sensitive to the accumulated historical wrongs and injustices that racial minorities, particularly blacks, have suffered in this society. Yet he does believe that the voluntariness of minorities who have strived to be included constitutes a substantial mitigating factor in any assessment of the cost they have incurred for inclusion.

What, then, should be the conception of American society that guides the formulation and implementation of public policy? Takaki and Glazer offer us two conceptually distinct but empirically intertwined possibilities. The color-blind society of Glazer, which places a premium on individual effort, right, responsibility and reward, is intertwined with the color-conscious society of Takaki, which sets the individual in the context of the group for the purpose of maximizing equity in the allotment of societal shares. Group entitlement serves to increase the chances of the individuals comprising it to win for themselves shares they might otherwise have been unable to appropriate, given a range of disadvantages—race, language, low social status, poor education, unfamiliarity with certain institutionalized social norms— in open brute competition of individuals qua individuals.

But does a color-conscious public policy run a terribly high risk of inequity and injustice to the individual qua individual in so far as group entitlement supercedes individual rights? Implicit in this question is the presumption that the risk of inequity and injustice of a color-conscious public policy is greater than that of a color-blind public policy, and it seems to ascribe moral superiority to a color-blind society over a color-conscious one.

This opens up a Pandora's box of problems that cannot be addressed here. Suffice it to say that the ontologies of the color-blind society and the color-conscious one sustain the moral superiority of neither. Empirically, one runs as much risk of occasioning inequity and injustice through a color-blind public policy as through a color-conscious one. The formulation and implementation of color-blind public policies with scrupulous fairness in a state of undue social inequalities must necessarily perputuate those inequalities. Ironically, it is color-conscious public policies that created many of the present undue social inequalities that color-blind public policies have allowed to persist. There is a most compelling paradox here. Color-conscious public policies gave rise to the demand for color-blind ones, which in turn have given rise to a new demand for color-conscious ones.

A story on the "CBS Evening News" of November 29, 1980, illustrates well the complexity of the color-blind/color-conscious public policy problem. The Desegregation Master of the Cleveland public school system had ordered the racial integration of the basketball teams in the system; each team had to have at least two white players. Many all-black teams were troubled, and some of their coaches were outraged by this decision. They contended that it is was a classic example of a well-intentioned color-conscious public policy run amuck, for the only proper way to select players for basketball teams is on the basis of individual ability and merit. They argued race and color should be irrelevant to the process of selection, which ought to be color-blind. Yet these same persons in a different context may argue just as vigorously for a color-conscious public policy in so far as they deem it to be in their interests.

The ideas of Takaki and Glazer are pivotal to our concerns, for the theoretical terms and the observational terms employed by each afford significantly different interpretations of the phenomena of race, ethnicity, and public policy in America. The other essays in this volume discuss selected aspects of public policy in relation to ethnicity and race.

What is the size of the ethnic/racial populations of America? This question is of no passing interest, as indicated in the decision of Federal District Judge Horace Gilmore—who agreed with the city of Detroit that its minority population had been seriously undercounted in the 1980 census, which could affect adversely the city's share of federal aid. Indeed, Judge Gilmore gave the federal government thirty days to come up with a plan for adjusting its count of the country's minority populations; this would add approximately five million persons to the population of the United States, using 1970 census data as the base. Ira Lowry's concern is with the extent to which the Census Bureau is capable of accurate large-scale identification of individuals who belong to a variety of ethnic groups, which presumably is essential to the Bureau's compliance with Judge Gilmore's order.

Lowry believes that the ethnic status of an individual is partly ascribed and partly achieved. It is "partly ascribed by his community from observation of his parentage, physical characteristics, language or mode of speech, organizational affiliations, and social circle. Some but not all these personal characteristics can be manipulated by the individual himself to reinforce or weaken the communal perception, so ethnicity is also partly an achieved status." The elements of ascription and achievement combine to make ethnicity an extremely fluid concept, making precise measurements of the ethnicity of individuals an immensely difficult task. Lowry believes the difficulty is compounded by the fact that "an individual may place either a positive or negative value on his ascribed ethnicity; and in either case may consider his ethnic identity to be important or unimportant." Moreover, "a particular ethnic identity may not be consistently ascribed by others even when they have access to the same information about the subject individual, and self-identification may differ from the communally ascribed status."

Lowry discusses in detail the technical aspects and the social significance of the problems accompanying ethnic self-identification in relation to the national census. His analysis leads him to the conclusion (expressed at the colloquium) that by scientific standards the 1980 census will be less than satisfactory in its count of the number and identity of individuals who comprise the society's various ethnic groups, and that politically the census will be quite problematic if one of its unintended consequences is the pitting of racial and/or ethnic minorities against one another for a variety of goods and services.

The problems of the census bear directly upon a problem identified in *Foreign Affairs* of Fall, 1980, as "a major issue 'on the rise'," namely, immigration. Roy Bryce-Laporte observes in his paper that the United States "is a country where history is defined conventionally as one of immigration and immigrants" and notes that it "is a society which persists in operating largely on the bases of ethnic distinctions and cultural differences, despite myths to the contrary." Given these basic beliefs about the society, he feels that "ethnicity, immigration and the relationship between them are irrefutably pertinent to any appreciation of the internal as well as external complexities of the contemporary United States." These are the core ideas that ground Bryce-Laporte's discussion of the public policy significance of what he terms "the new immigration."

This term covers the legal and illegal settlement of foreign-born nationals (expatriates) in the United States since the passage of the Immigration and Naturalization Act of 1965. The massive influx of persons over the past decade has become a major issue and problem in public policy, leading to the creation of the Select Commission on Immigration in 1978 by the Congress, which charged it under Public Law 95-412 with evaluating the current laws, policies, and practices pertaining to the admission of immigrants and refugees to the United States, and recommending appropriate changes to the President and the Congress. The figures cited by Bryce-Laporte call attention to the size of the recent migration to the United States, but more important than size are the phenotypic and socio-cultural attributes of the groups and individuals who have entered. They are, for the most part, *highly visible.* Bryce-Laporte discusses in detail the social and public policy significance of phenotypic, linguistic, and cultural visibility in America.

The new immigrants from countries such as Mexico, the Philippines, Korea, China-Taiwan, the Dominican Republic, and Jamaica are highly visible in the context of what Robert Rhodes, a former colleague of mine at Ohio University, terms the "abstract white majority." The term denotes the presence of empirically sufficient phenotypic attributes to make an individual count and be treated as a part of the society's white majority. There are, of course, clear and distinct differences among abstractly white individuals and groups, but these are irrelevant to their social visibility. Racial majority status is thus conferred on groups and individuals who are abstractly white, making them invisible. The social value of this invisibility may be diminished by high linguistic and cultural visibility, but the cost of this can be moderated by behaviors that are consistent with the constitutive and generative principles of the social order, as well as the traditions of the majority with which they are identified.

Given the strong inclusivist impulse of this society for those who are abstractly white, new immigrants with high linguistic and cultural visibility but low phenotypic visibility are better positioned to penetrate the structure of social relationships that foster security, status, and prestige than those who are highly visible phenotypically, regardless of the low linguistic and cultural visibility they might evince. The importance of this point is demonstrated well by Bryce-Laporte's discussion of new immigrants who are abstractly white and those who are black, Oriental, or Latin-American.

New immigrants make demands upon the resources of the society to which they contribute materially, culturally, and spiritually. Yet many perceive an imbalance between the contributions of the new immigrants and the demands they make upon the society's resources, particularly in this epoch of stagflation, huge budget deficits, low productivity, and low rates of growth. Bryce-Laporte takes strong issue with those who use the present difficulties of the society's political economy as a springboard for stirring anti-immigration sentiments in the populace. He is scathing in comments concerning those academics whose works provide conceptual and empirical reinforcement for the anti-immigration sentiments abroad in the country. He observes that what is needed at this time is neither hysteria nor camouflaged advocacy to legitimize policy grounded in the baser elements of self-interest, but instead calm and dispassionate analysis of the conceptual, analytical, and empirical links between local, national, and international public policies impelling peoples throughout the world towards resettlement in the United States.

Many of those who have sought resettlement in the United States are covered by the umbrella term "Hispanic." The size of this population increased approximately sixty percent during the decade of the 1970s from roughly seven million to twelve million persons. It has been estimated that if present trends were to continue, the Hispanic population should be larger than the black population by the turn of the century. This development would no doubt affect significantly the form and content of social services now used by both populations.

The use of social services subjects one to the terms of their delivery — criteria of eligibility, limits of benefits, etc. — and the accompanying social control. Adalberto Aguirre, Jr., discusses what may be called the logic of control of social services delivery. The logic of control entails the empirical context in which the rational manipulation of the elements of a particular structure determines its behavior. Aguirre believes that the political manipulation of social services is designed to control the behaviors of their recipients.

Reflecting upon the impact of social services on the Hispanic population, Aguirre is concerned that "the increasing heterogeniety of the Hispanic community may prompt the use of social services as a reward system. Given the fact that social services are subject to political manipulation, it may be possible, and highly rational, to use social services to reward that element in the Hispanic population with the

weakest political potential." This would no doubt foster severe cleav-
ages in the Hispanic population, emasculate its political strength, and
undermine the development of effective coalitions among the diverse
groups that compose it. This would be disastrous for the well-being of
the collective, even though it may be advantageous to particular individuals and groups within it. Aguirre believes that the collective interests of the Hispanic population require action(s) designed to limit, if
not prevent, the creation of debilitating factions within it by social
services bureaucracies. This necessitates effective participation by
Hispanics in the delivery of social services.

Effective participation in any form of organized human activity is
empirically impossible if one neither knows nor understands the terms
of the language in which it is structured. The ability to understand the
sentences of a given language, interpret the facts they signify, and determine the values they present is crucial if one is to participate effectively in the activity that uses the language. Put differently, individuals in the Hispanic population, or any other population for that
matter, who are unable to interpret the facts and determine the values
that ground the delivery of social services, cannot participate effectively in the organization of these activities.

Aguirre is most sensitive to the empirical significance of this point,
and so he argues strongly for the systematic inclusion of the Spanish
language into the structure of the social services system. He is mindful
of the fact that a knowledge of the language of social services, in all its
complexities and subtleties, is a necessary but *not* a sufficient condition for effective individual and community participation in the delivery of social services to the Hispanic population. Still, it is his conviction that the "bilingualization" of social services, if we may so speak,
should improve in some measure their quality, as well as make Hispanics more alert to their faction-creating potentialities. It is vital, Aguirre
believes, that Hispanics become conscious of the fact that social services are not designed to nurture the growth of a strong and purposeful
political economy within the Hispanic community, but, as is true of
their purpose in other communities, to keep it/them dependent economically and enfeebled politically. This consciousness should impel
them to take those forms of action necessary to the realization of their
common interests.

If Aguirre is troubled by the state and effects of social services in the
Hispanic community, Carl Tahkofper expresses deep distress with
the present state of affairs of Native American reservations in the
West, particularly the exploitation of the land for mineral resources. It
is truly one of the profound ironies of history that the very land to
which the Native American was driven by his European conquerer in

xiv

the belief that it was worthless should turn out to possess some of the largest deposits of coal, oil and gas, and uranium in the country. The critical need of our technitronic society for these sources of energy is too obvious to belabor here.

Tahkofper desires to maximize the use of the reservations' resources for the benefit and well-being of their inhabitants, but he is appalled at how Native American lands are currently treated. He discusses key contributory factors to, and effects of, this unhealthy situation. Unless decisive action is taken soon, Tahkofper believes that given the tremendous pressure being exerted on tribes by government officials as well as by private entrepreneurs to exploit the resources of their lands—and given the trend of long-term leases running well into the twenty-first century that are being signed—Native Americans will all but have lost the battle to determine their own destinies in the context of life on the reservations. What will become of the Native American youth if this trend persists? Tahkofper believes that the dependency of the next generation on agencies outside the boundaries of the reservations will be even greater than that of the present one—a dependency that traps the Native American between two worlds, both tugging and pulling at him but neither really nurturing the actualization of his inherent potentialities. In a very real and unsettling way, the exclusivist tradition of which Takaki speaks seems very applicable to the Native American living on a reservation.

The force of America's exclusivist tradition was once nowhere more obvious than in the composition of the armed forces. Racial minorities were excluded systematically from all but the least attractive roles. A gradual change in this state of affairs marked the period from the issuance of President Truman's Executive Order, which integrated the armed forces, to the beginning of America's large-scale involvement in Vietnam. The period of the Vietnam War to the present is noted for a rather sharp increase in the number of individuals from racial minorities, particularly blacks, who have joined the armed forces either voluntarily or involuntarily. Today all who serve in the armed forces do so voluntarily, and many are concerned about its racial composition as well as its fighting ability. In these pages Charles Moskos looks at one branch of the armed forces, the Army, in order to discern the social and military significance of its racial and educational composition.

He notes that in 1979 "blacks accounted for 28.9 percent of the Army, 19.8 percent of the Marine Corps, 13.8 percent of the Air Force, and 9.7 percent of the Navy." The rising percentage of blacks in the military "has generated more heat than any other topic in the debate on the all-volunteer force." The Army is increasingly unrepresentative of the population as a whole, and Moskos observes that "white reluctance to join an increasingly black organization" contributes to this, although admitting the precise degree is unknown. The size of the black presence in the Army, disproportionately large in relation to the society's black population, troubles many who question the fairness of any one group bearing a disproportionate share of the burden to fight and die defending what is termed the entire country's interests. This matter of fairness aside, there is another troublesome and disquieting concern shared by many: Will the black foot soldier equip himself well in combat *regardless* of the field of battle?

Moskos is not as troubled as many by the size of the black presence in the Army, but he is alarmed by the growing under-representation of America's middle class in it. From Moskos' vantage point, the Army is not an increasingly black one but an army of the underclass. Given the large middle class comprising most of America's society (Aristotle would be pleased were he alive), Moskos is distressed by trends which show the Army becoming less and less representative of this class.

Class, not race, is the pivot of the Army's manpower problems, he argues. "I am unpersuaded," says Moskos, "that any significant number of middle class whites—or middle class of any race, for that matter—would be more likely to join the Army under present recruitment incentives, even if the Army were overwhelmingly white." This is a very important point, for it focuses attention on incentives which have had the effect of debasing the Army by education even as they have diversified it by race. Contrary to the belief of many, the sizeable presence of blacks in the Army is not the efficient cause of its debased education, for "since the end of the draft, the proportion of black high school graduates entering the Army has exceeded that of whites, and this is a trend that is becoming more pronounced."

The end of conscription has been accompanied by a significant decrease in the number of college graduates, black and white, as well as white high school graduates in the Army. Black high school graduates often perceive the Army as a means of upward social mobility. Thus the social forces that have fostered the inclusion of blacks have tended to encourage the exclusion of whites. Moskos observes that "the all-volunteer force as presently constituted has come to exclude enlisted participation by those who will be America's future leaders, whether in government, business, or the intellectual and academic communities." To rectify this state of affairs, he favors the institution of "workable conscription." He believes that a national consensus concerning its need, in addition to attractive educational incentives, could make a return to conscription both generally acceptable and workable.

Moskos desires a workable conscription for the sake of the common

xvi

good. But it is no easy matter to effect the convergence of various interests and purposes into the common good, which is the good of all collectively, not the good of each individually. Each person may not benefit from the common good in every instance, but all benefit from it in the totality of particular instances. The essays in this volume are concerned fundamentally with the common good in their discussions of ethnicity, race, and public policy. They invite one to map for oneself the relations between the interests and purposes of individuals and groups and the common good. This is not easy, for the essays do not present a form of the common good that everyone can agree upon. One need not despair in this, however, for the pure Form of the common good, like Plato's Republic, is set in the heavens or in human yearning and is not amenable to empirical observation and demonstration. Still, its value is inestimable, for it provides a guide to human conduct in the struggle of our species to maximize its inherent potentialities through social intercourse.

The first fruit of any labor is often the most difficult to realize. This volume is the first fruit of the labor of the University of Wisconsin System American Ethnic Studies Coordinating Committee's Annual Green Bay Colloquium on "Ethnicity and Public Policy." The labor of many individuals made the first colloquium possible, and we thank them all. We should, however, be remiss if we were not to give a very special word of thanks to Thomas V. Tonnesen, the committee's program coordinator, whose hard work and sound judgment made the colloquium's fruition all the easier, and whose editorial assistance was invaluable in the preparation of this volume. We should also like to thank W. Werner Prange, the former director of the University of Wisconsin Urban Corridor Consortium, under the auspices of which the committee falls, for his imaginative and tireless support of the committee's interests and purposes in the higher councils of the university.

Reflections on Racial Patterns in America: An Historical Perspective

Ronald Takaki

University of California, Berkeley

The *raison d'être* of this colloquium on "Ethnicity and Public Policy" can be stated simply—racial inequality is still a ubiquitous reality in American society. There are, of course, different perceptions of this reality as well as different prescriptions for solving the problem. One purpose of our meeting is to give us an opportunity to subject both our perceptions and prescriptions to rigorous and critical scrutiny

The need for such scrutiny has recently become a topic of much discussion in California, particularly among University of California administrators. (A few months ago, they learned that 56 percent of California public school students in grades K-12 will be black, Hispanic, and Asian by 1990.) This shift in the racial composition of the population will be evident even earlier. Within five years, Asians will comprise 8 percent of all graduating high school seniors, blacks 10 percent, Hispanics 25 percent, and Native Americans 1 percent. Together, minority students will amount to 44 percent of the total number of high school graduates in 1985. For the first time in the history of the university, administrators find themselves facing the question: What is the institution's responsibility to this increasing minority population projected to become a majority in the state? These demographic changes, which reflect a general growth of the nation's minority population, underscore the centrality of race as a public policy issue in American society during the next decade.[1]

As an historian, I should like to suggest that we begin our discussion of the problems of racial inequality in the 1980s from an historical perspective. As you may know, I have recently completed a study of racism, *Iron Cages: Race and Culture in 19th Century America.* But for our dialogue, I should like to offer some reflections on another historical study—an essay written by Nathan Glazer on "The Emergence of an American Ethnic Pattern," published as chapter one in his book *Affirmative Discrimination: Ethnic Inequality and Public Policy.*[2]

Published in 1975, *Affirmative Discrimination* is a forthright statement against affirmative action policies. Excerpts from reviews quoted on the back cover of the 1978 paperback edition are intended to do more than announce its importance; they warn us not to ignore the book. I shall cite three of them:

> A tempered, factually argued, vigorous polemic against the predominant drift of public policy on racial issues over the past decade. Public issues only infrequently receive serious, sustained arguments of this high order.
> *The New York Times Book Review*
>
> Glazer writes provocatively, instead of ideologically, about a sensitive subject that needs airing.
> *Business Week*
>
> His views, based on solid research, deserve the widest debate.
> *The Christian Science Monitor* [3]

As the excerpts suggest, the book has more than a scholarly purpose. Indeed, as Glazer himself makes clear in his 1978 Introduction, he is seeking to influence public policies makers, particularly the justices of the Supreme Court in their deliberations on affirmative action cases such as the Allan Bakke Case. "In *Affirmative Discrimination*," he writes, "I attacked the justice and the wisdom of shifting from individual rights to group rights in devising policies to overcome racial and ethnic-group discrimination and its heritage." While Glazer claims that he has "no intention of 'predicting' the course of the Supreme Court," he describes the courts as the "final battleground" for the issue of affirmative action and encourages Americans who share his "vision to engage in litigation and submit amicus briefs against the new policies." In short, *Affirmative Discrimination* is Glazer's amicus brief.[4]

His book requires our attention. We could, I think, avoid his book if it were only an empirical study of employment, education and housing. But his analysis also advances a theory of an "American ethnic pattern" to interpret American history and to influence present public policy making.[5]

At the heart of Glazer's theory is a hope, a vision of a good society in which "men and women are judged on the basis of their abilities rather than their color, race, or ethnic origin." The "first principle of a liberal society," he insists, is the assertion that "the individual and the individual's interests and good and welfare are the test of a good society." Thus for Glazer, there is only one proper solution to the problem of racial inequality: the heritage of discrimination can and should be overcome by "simply attacking discrimination."[6]

A theoretician of the anti-affirmative action backlash, Glazer gives articulation to an angry popular mood, a widespread resentment against the demands of racial minorities, and a moral outrage felt by the Allan Bakkes of America. He both describes and supports the point of view of the white ethnics: "They entered a society in which they were scorned; they nevertheless worked hard, they received little or no support from government or public agencies, their children received no special attention in school or special opportunity to attend college. . . . They contrast their situation with that of blacks and other minority groups today and see substantial differences in treatment. They consider themselves patriotic and appreciative of the United States even though they received no special benefit." While Glazer admits the comparison may be "crude and unfair," he essentially agrees with its main contention, that blacks and other racial minorities should not receive "special" opportunities, "special" treatment, and "special" benefits. Instead, they should emulate the example of the white ethnics.[7]

In his opening chapter, "The Emergence of an American Ethnic Pattern," Glazer develops the historical and theoretical underpinnings of his critique of affirmative action policies. He uses this to provide the conceptual framework for the entire book and refers to its main points throughout the study. Viewing affirmative action policies from his historical perspective, Glazer asks at the end of the book: "How have policies which so sharply reverse the consensus developed over two hundred years of American history established themselves so powerfully in a scant ten years?"[8]

But what was that "consensus" which had developed over two hundred years? According to Glazer, the mid-1960s witnessed the emergence of a "national consensus" on solutions to the problems of racial and ethnic prejudice. This consensus was reflected in three laws: the Civil Rights Act of 1964; the Voting Rights Act of 1965; and the Immigration Act of 1965. Essentially these laws prohibited discrimination based on race, color, religion, or national origin. But "paradoxically," Glazer argues, a new policy of affirmative action or "discrimination" was then instituted, and the consensus was "broken." Thus was shattered the "culmination" of the development of a "distinctive American orientation of ethnic difference and diversity with a history of almost 200 years."[9]

Glazer bases his theory of an American ethnic pattern on three historical developments or "decisions":

First, the entire world would be allowed to enter the United States. The claim that some nations or races were to be favored in entry over others was, for a while, accepted, but it was eventually rejected. And once having entered into the United States—and whether that entry was by means of forced enslavement, free immigration, or conquest—all citizens would have equal rights. No group would be considered subordinate to another.

Second, no separate ethnic group was to be allowed to establish an independent polity in the United States. This was to be a union of states and a nation of free individuals, not a nation of politically defined ethnic groups.

Third, no group, however, would be required to give up its group character and distinctiveness as the price of full entry into the American society and polity.

All three decisions were inclusionist rather than exclusionist. Though a notion favoring the entry of particular immigrants or races was accepted "for a while," American society eventually allowed the inclusion of all racial and ethnic groups. The decisions were also egalitarian: all citizens, regardless of race, ethnicity, or religion, would have equal rights. These decisions also promoted tolerance and acceptance of cultural and ethnic diversity: a group would be allowed to maintain its cultural values and identity. Finally, all three decisions minimized, even denied, differences between the experiences of "racial" and white "ethnic" groups in American history.[10]

While Glazer describes the three decisions as integral parts of the "central" American pattern, he does acknowledge the existence of contrary "actions"—black slavery, anti-immigrant nativism, the "near extermination" of the American Indian, the lynching of Chinese, the relocation of Japanese Americans during World War II, and so forth. He even notes that, "for fifty years, between the 1890s and the 1930s, exclusivism was dominant." Nevertheless, for Glazer all of these contrary developments do not represent the "large direction," the "major tendency to a greater inclusiveness," in American history.[11]

Thus the three decisions are claimed to be major components of historical reality in America, and as an historian I had to ask whether the claim could stand the test of a rigorous and critical examination of the historical evidence. More specifically, I had to ask whether Glazer's theory of an American "ethnic" pattern could explain the history of racial minorities in America.

The first is the most important of all three decisions, for it permitted the "entire" world to enter the United States and extended "equal" rights to all citizens regardless of their means of entry. In order for us to determine whether this decision actually existed historically and whether it represented a major pattern, we need to review the history of citizenship and the right of suffrage in the United

States. We also need to develop a more precise chronological measurement of how long "for a while" really was.[12]

The phrase "for a while" could refer to the early national period, when the United States Congress made its first effort to define American citizenship in the Naturalization Law of 1790. This law specified that only free "white" immigrants would be eligible for naturalized citizenship. Clearly, this law did not allow the "entire" world to enter the United States as potential citizens or members of the body politic. Non-"white" immigrants were not permitted to be naturalized until the Walter-McCarran Act of 1952, which stated that "the right of a person to become a naturalized citizen of the United States shall not be denied or abridged because of race. . . ." What is important to note here about the first naturalization law is the fact that it remained in effect for 162 years, or for a very long time.[13]

One of the first laws to be passed by Congress, the Naturalization Law of 1790 acquired special significance in the nineteenth century due to westward expansionism and the entry of Chinese laborers into America. The two developments were closely linked. Shortly after the end of the war against Mexico, which enabled the United States to annex California, Aaron H. Palmer, a "Counsellor of the Supreme Court of the United States," submitted to Congress a plan for the extension of American markets into Asia and the importation of Chinese workers to develop American industries. "The commodious port of San Francisco," he declared, "is destined to become the great emporium of our commerce on the Pacific; and so soon as it is connected by railroad with the Atlantic States, will become the most eligible point of departure for steamers to . . . China." To build the transcontinental railroad as well as to bring the "fertile lands of California" under cultivation, Palmer recommended the immigration of Chinese. Here, in this remarkable report, was a public policy blueprint which explicitly integrated American expansion into Asia with Asiatic immigration to America.[14]

During the next three decades, tens of thousands of Chinese were recruited to work in this country. Between 1850 and 1880, the Chinese population in the United States increased from 7,520 to 105,465, a fifteen-fold increase; in 1870 the Chinese constituted 8.6 percent of the total population of California and an impressive 25 percent of the wage-earning force. But the inclusion of the Chinese in the economic structure was accompanied by their political exclusion. Not "white," they were ineligible for naturalized citizenship. They were, in effect, migrant laborers, forced to be foreigners forever. Unlike white "ethnic" immigrants such as Italians, Poles, and Irish, the Chinese were a politically proscribed labor force. They were a part of America's production process but not her body politic. American businessmen expected them to be here only on a temporary basis and located them in a racially segmented labor market. Central Pacific Railroad employer Charles Crocker, for example, told a legislative committee: "I do not believe they are going to remain here long enough to become good citizens, and I would not admit them to citizenship." Crocker also explained how the presence of Chinese workers could elevate white workers in a stratified racial/occupational structure: "I believe that the effect of Chinese labor upon white labor has an elevating instead of degrading tendency. I think that every white man who is intelligent and able to work, who is more than a digger in a ditch . . . who has the capacity of being something else, can get to be something else by the presence of Chinese labor easier than he could without it. . . There is proof of that in the fact that after we got the Chinamen to work, we took the more intelligent of the white laborers and made foremen of them." Businessmen "availed" themselves of this "unlimited" supply of "cheap" Chinese labor to build their railroads and operate their factories. After the Chinese migrant workers had completed their service, they were urged to return to their homeland, while others came to replace them. The employers of Chinese labor did not want these workers to remain in this country and become "thick" (to use Crocker's term) in American society.[15]

Enacted long before the entry of Asians into America, the Naturalization Law also had another consequence for immigrants from the East. Where white "ethnic" immigrants were legally entitled to own land in this country, Asian immigrants were subjected to a special form of discrimination. Defined as "aliens ineligible for citizenship," Chinese and other Asian immigrants were also denied, by state legislation, the right to own property in California, Washington, Arizona, Oregon, Idaho, Nebraska, Texas, Kansas, Louisiana, Montana, New Mexico, Minnesota, and Missouri. Thus Asian immigrants were excluded from the very process of land ownership, social mobility, and transformation of immigrants into Americans which Frederick Jackson Turner celebrated in his famous essay on the significance of the frontier in American history.[16]

Ironically, the Naturalization Law also excluded Native Americans from citizenship. Though they were born in the United States, they were regarded as members of tribes, or as domestic subjects or nationals; their status was considered analogous to children of foreign diplomats born here. As "foreigners," they could not seek naturalized citizenship, for they were not "white." Even the Fourteenth Amendment, which defined federal citizenship, did not apply to Native Americans. While Native Americans could become United

States citizens through treaties with specific tribes or through allotment programs such as the Dawes Act of 1887, general citizenship for the original American was not granted until 1924.[17]

But what happened to non-white citizens? Did they have "equal" rights, particularly the right of suffrage? Citizenship did not necessarily carry this right, for states determined the requirements for voting. A review of this history reveals a basic political inequality between white citizens and non-white citizens.

The 1965 Voting Rights Act did not actually culminate a history of political inclusion for blacks. In the North, during the most important period of political inclusion—the era of Jacksonian Democracy—the establishment of universal manhood suffrage was for white men only. In reality, the inclusion of greater numbers of white men, including recent Irish immigrants, was usually accompanied by the exclusion of black citizens from the suffrage. The New York Constitution of 1821, for example, granted the vote to all free "white" male citizens who possessed a freehold, paid taxes, had served in the state militia, or had worked on the highways; it also retained the property requirement for black citizens, increasing it from $100 to $250. The Pennsylvania Constitution of 1838 went even further: it provided for universal "white" manhood suffrage and thus disfranchised black citizens completely. In the South, except for a brief period during Reconstruction, black citizens were systematically excluded from participation in the political process. Thus the 1965 law, enacted in response to massive black pressure and protest under the leadership of Martin Luther King, was a break from a long history of denial of voting rights to racial as opposed to "ethnic" minority citizens.[18]

This difference between race and ethnicity in terms of the suffrage may also be seen in the experiences of Native Americans. While the Treaty of Guadalupe-Hidalgo had offered United States citizenship to Mexicans living within the acquired territories, the 1849 Constitution of California granted the right of suffrage only to every "white" male citizen of the United States and only to every "white" male citizen of Mexico who had elected to become a United States citizen. A color line, in short, had been drawn for the granting of suffrage to American citizens in California. Native Americans were also proscribed politically in other states. The Fifteenth Amendment, which provided that the right to vote shall not be denied or abridged because of race or color, did not apply to non-citizen Indians. Even after Indians were granted citizenship under the 1924 law, however, many of them were designated "Indians not taxed" or "persons under guardianship" and disfranchised in states like Arizona, New Mexico, Idaho, and Washington.[19]

Our study of the history of citizenship and the suffrage disclosed a racial and exclusionist pattern. For 162 years, the naturalization law, while allowing various European or "white" ethnic groups to enter the United States and acquire citizenship, specifically denied citizenship to other groups on a racial basis. While the suffrage was extended to white men, it was withheld from men of color. Thus what actually developed historically in American society was a pattern of citizenship and suffrage which drew a very sharp distinction between "ethnicity" and "race."

Like the first one, the second and third decisions also require our critical examination. According to Glazer, all Americans would be viewed and treated as "free individuals," not members of "politically defined ethnic groups" or "polities." Still, Americans could, if they wished, maintain an ethnic group identity on a voluntary basis. They would be allowed to have their distinctive religion, their own language, their own schools, and even to maintain their "loyalty" to their "old country."[20]

While decisions two and three may have been true for white "ethnic" groups like the Irish and Germans, they certainly do not accurately describe the historical experiences of "racial" groups. This difference was particularly evident during World War II when Japanese Americans, unlike German Americans and Italian Americans, were forcefully interned in relocation camps. They were, in effect, defined and treated as a "polity" by the federal government. Of the 120,000 internees, 70,000 were United States citizens by right of birth. Japanese in America were not regarded as "free individuals" but as members of a polity simply because of their Japanese ancestry. In the camps, draft-age Nisei men were required to fill out and sign a loyalty questionnaire entitled "Statement of United States Citizenship of Japanese Ancestry." At the end of the long list of questions, they were asked:

> No. 27. Are you willing to serve in the armed forces of the United States on combat duty wherever ordered?

> No. 28. Will you swear unqualified allegiance to the United States of America and faithfully defend the United States from any or all attack by foreign or domestic forces, and forswear any form of allegiance or obedience to the Japanese emperor, to any other foreign government, power or organization?

Young men of Italian or German ancestry were not subject to such a "loyalty" test.[21]

The Native American experience also does not fit well into decisions two and three. Indians have historically been formally treated as members of polities, not as "free individuals." The Constitution of the

United States recognized Indian tribes as polities: Article I, Section 2, excluded from state representation in Congress "Indians not taxed;" and Article I, Section 4, granted Congress the power to "regulate Commerce with foreign Nations . . . and with Indian Tribes." The Indian Trade and Intercourse Act of 1802 provided that no land cessions in Indian territory could be made except by "treaty" between Congress and the Indian tribe. The view of Indian tribes as polities was explicitly expressed in the 1871 case of *McKay v. Campbell*. Denying the Fourteenth Amendment had extended citizenship to Indians, the court ruled:

> To be a citizen of the United States by reason of his birth, a person must not only be born within its territorial limits, but he must also be born subject to its jurisdiction. . . . But the Indian tribes within the limits of the United States have always been held to be distinct and independent political communities, retaining the right of self-government, though subject to the protecting power of the United States.

The removal of Choctaws, Creeks, and Cherokees in the 1830s and the relocation of Sioux and Cheyennes on reservations in the 1870s were also based on the conception of Indian tribes as polities.[22]

This policy of defining Indians as members of tribes and as members of culturally distinct groups was used as a means to control them. The strategy can be seen in the actions of two important policy makers on Indian affairs. President Andrew Jackson, claiming Indians were culturally distinct and could not survive in white civilization, proposed their removal beyond the Mississippi River. Regarding Indian tribes as polities, Jackson was able to negotiate removal treaties with them and to transfer Indian lands into the "markett," to use the President's spelling. As Commissioner of Indian Affairs in 1872, Francis Amasa Walker saw that he could not continue Jackson's policy of removing Indians beyond the Mississippi River. By then the "markett" had already reached the Pacific Ocean, and a new future for the Indian in the West had to be defined. Walker's proposal was to "consolidate" Indian tribes onto one or two "grand reservations." According to his plan, warlike tribes would be relocated on extensive tracts in the West, and all Indian "bands" outside of the reservation would be "liable to be struck by the military at any time, without warning, and without any implied hostility to those members of the tribe" living within the reservation. For Walker, it was a policy of military convenience to treat Indian tribes as polities.[23]

Yet, it must be noted, federal Indian policies were not entirely consistent. At times they also reflected an inclusionist pattern. Even Walker's reservation system was designed to "civilize" Indians and prepare them for entry into American white society. His proposal would enable the federal government to extend over Indians what Walker called "a rigid reformatory discipline." The crucial term is reformatory. On the reservations Indians would be trained, "required" to learn the arts of industry and placed on a course of "self-improvement." Not allowed to "escape work," Indians would be helped over the rough places on "the white man's road." Furthermore, some federal policies prohibited the recognition of Indian tribes as independent polities in the United States. The Indian Appropriation Act of 1871, for example, provided that "hereafter no Indian nation or tribe within the territory of the United States shall be acknowledged or recognized as an independent nation, tribe, or power, with whom the United States may contract by treaty." But the aim of this law was not to recognize Indians as "free individuals" but to reduce tribal power and give railroad corporations access to Indian lands and right-of-way through Indian territory.[24]

Federal inclusionist policies also required the Indian to give up his group character and distinctiveness as the "price" of full entry into American society and polity. Nowhere can this be seen more clearly than in the Dawes Act of 1887, also known as the Indian Allotment Act. This law, which white reformers hailed as the "Indian Emancipation Act," promised to bring to a close a "century of dishonor." What it actually did was to grant the president power, at his discretion and without the Indians' consent, to break up reservations and allot lands to individual Indians. The Dawes Act also permitted the federal government to secure tribal consent to sell "surplus" reservation lands—lands which remained after allotment had taken place—to white settlers. The effect of this policy on the Indian land base was predictable. Between 1887 and 1934, when the allotment policy was terminated, sixty percent of the Indian land base had been transferred to whites, 60,000,000 acres had been sold as "surplus" lands to whites by the federal government, and 27,000,000 acres—or two-thirds of the land allotted to individual Indians—had been transferred to whites through private transactions. This tremendous reduction of the Indian land base has had a very destructive impact on Native American cultures—their distinctive religions, languages, and ethnic group identities. The law also conferred citizenship upon the allottees and any other Indians who would abandon their tribes and adopt the "habits of civilized life." Thus the Dawes Act, offering Indians entry, exacted a "price."[25]

Still, Glazer insists that the history of American society in relation to its many groups is "not a history of racism," and he lines up three authorities to back his claim: Yehoshua Arieli, Hans Kohn, and Seymour Martin Lipset.[26]

Arieli's main point in his *Individualism and Nationalism in American Ideology* supports Glazer's inclusionist hypothesis. The American experience, according to Arieli, has emphasized individualism, egalitarianism, and freedom rather than ethnic or racial group characteristics and limitations. He traces these ideas back to the founding fathers, noting that "citizenship was the only criterion which made the individual a member of the national community." As paraphrased by Glazer, Arieli claims that many of those who "founded and helped define the nation" rejected "ethnic exclusivity."[27]

He acknowledges, however, the existence of a tradition of exclusionism, and cites Benjamin Franklin as an example of this. As quoted by Glazer, Arieli points out how Franklin "strenuously argued against the wisdom of permitting the immigration of non-English settlers, who 'will never adopt our language or customs anymore than they can acquire our complexion'." Glazer then adds, Franklin was "undoubtedly" influenced by the substantial number of Germans in Pennsylvania. If we go to the original source of Franklin's statement as quoted in Arieli, we will find that it was taken from Franklin's essay on "Observations Concerning the Increase of Mankind." A reading of this essay will quickly reveal that Franklin's deeper concern was based on race. He observed that the number of "purely white People" in the world was proportionately very small. All Africa was black or tawny, Asia chiefly tawny, and "America (exclusive of the new comers) wholly so." The English were the "principle Body of white People," and Franklin wished there were more of them in America. "And while we are . . . Scouring our Planet, by clearing America of Woods, and so making this Side of our globe reflect a brighter Light to the Eyes of Inhabitants in Mars or Venus," he declared, "why should we in the Sight of Superior Beings, darken its People? why increase the Sons of Africa, by Planting them in America, where we have so fair an opportunity, by excluding Blacks and Tawneys, of increasing the lovely White. . . ?"[28]

Still, it can be argued, as does Glazer, that Franklin's was a "private" comment to be set against a "public" one which proclaimed America "a place of refuge." Arieli emphasizes this larger American purpose and quotes Alexis de Tocqueville to illustrate this theme of an inclusionist American nationality. Writing to a friend, the perspicacious French visitor exclaimed:

> Picture to yourself . . . if you can, a society which comprises all the nations of the world . . . people differing from one another in language, in beliefs, in opinions; in a word a society possessing no

roots, no memories, no prejudices, no routine, no common ideas, no national character, yet with a happiness a hundred times greater than our own. . . . This, then, is our starting point. What is the connecting link between these so different elements? How are they welded into one people?[29]

Curiously, Arieli discusses American citizenship without a single reference to the Naturalization Law of 1790, which limited naturalized citizenship to a particular racial group. Moreover, he quotes Tocqueville very selectively. Actually, what the astute Frenchman found striking in American society was not only the "general equality of condition" but also the fact that this condition was reserved for white men only. As he travelled through America, he noticed how blacks had been reduced to slaves in the South and pariahs in the North and how Indians were the victims of removal and genocide. Describing Northern racial segregation, Tocqueville wrote:

The same schools do not receive the children of the black and the European. In the theaters gold cannot procure a seat for the servile race beside their former masters; in the hospitals they lie apart; and although they are allowed to invoke the same God as the whites, it must be at a different altar and in their own churches, with their own clergy. The gates of heaven are not closed against them, but their inferiority is continued to the very confines of the other world. When the Negro dies, his bones are cast aside, and the distinction of condition prevails even in the equality of death.

And witnessing a band of Choctaws driven westward by United States soldiers, Tocqueville reported:

It was then the middle of winter, and the cold was unusually severe; the snow had frozen hard upon the ground, and the river was drifting huge masses of ice. The Indians had their families with them, and they brought in their train the wounded and the sick, with children newly born and old men upon the verge of death.

What awed Tocqueville was the ability of white society to deprive the Indians of their rights and exterminate them "with singular felicity, tranquilly, legally, philanthropically. . . ." As he caught a glimpse of a peculiar horror present in an American racial pattern, he remarked in barbed language: "It is impossible to destroy men with more respect for the laws of humanity."[30]

Tocqueville's observations on racial inequality were neither cursory nor isolated comments in his writings. In fact, they are interspersed throughout his two-volume study *Democracy in America,* and the last chapter of Volume I is a 109-page assessment of "The Present and Probable Future Condition of the Three Races That Inhabit the

Territory of the United States." In this chapter Tocqueville offered a grim prognosis of the pattern of race in America: "The European is to the other races of mankind what man himself is to the lower animals: he makes them subservient to his use, and when he cannot subdue he destroys them." Thus Tocqueville predicted that the Indians would perish as whites expanded their civilization westward, and blacks would continue to be kept subordinate and "fastened" to whites "without intermingling."[31]

How do we account for Arieli's glaring oversights—his failure to note the first naturalization law and Tocqueville's critical assessment of racism in America? One reason, I think, is a tendency to meld together ethnicity and race—to use both terms interchangeably as if they were the same. Hans Kohn in *American Nationalism* also seems to make this mistake. Consequently, he asserts that the "first sharp restriction of immigration" occurred in the 1920s. It would have been impossible for Kohn to have written such a statement unless he were ignorant of the 1882 Chinese Exclusion Act, which was the first immigration restriction law, or unless he viewed immigration wholly in relation to European or white "ethnics." In his chapter on "A Nation of Many Nations," Kohn is really studying ethnicity, not race, but he does not differentiate between the two.[32]

The most revealing example of this confusion is Kohn's discussion of Thomas Jefferson and the founding father's conception of America as a "sanctuary" and a "Canaan." Here we have a situation where Glazer draws from Kohn to requote Jefferson and repeats Kohn's claim that Jefferson viewed America as a "universal nation," composed of "many ethnic strains." If we trace the source of the quotation, we will find that Kohn took it from Jefferson's letter to George Flower, written on September 12, 1817, and published in Volume VII of *The Writings of Thomas Jefferson,* edited by H. A. Washington. If we examine the entire letter, we will plainly see that Jefferson was actually referring to white "ethnic" immigrants— Swiss, French, and Germans. Within this context, then, America was a "sanctuary" for white immigrants fleeing from the "misrule of Europe."[33]

If we browse through Volume VII of Jefferson's *Writings,* we will come across uncontestable proof that Jefferson's inclusionism was for white ethnics only. In a letter to Doctor Thomas Humphreys, dated February 8, 1817, Jefferson supported a proposal for the removal of free blacks to Africa. "Perhaps the proposition now on the carpet at Washington to provide an establishment on the coast of Africa for voluntary emigrations of peoples of color," Jefferson wrote, "may be the corner stone of this future edifice." Thus when Jefferson discussed in his letter to Flower, written only several months later, the "quicker amalgamation" of new settlers, he was restricting this process to white ethnic groups.[34]

Though Jefferson was the owner of two hundred slaves, he advocated the abolition of slavery and the removal of blacks from America. He believed that blacks and whites could never coexist in America because of "the real distinctions" which "nature" had made between the two races. "The first difference which strikes us is that of color," Jefferson explained. "And is this difference of no importance? Is it not the foundation of a greater or less share of beauty in the two races? Are not the fine mixtures of red and white, the expressions of every passion by greater or less suffusions of color in the one, preferable to that eternal monotony, which reigns in the countenances, that immovable veil of black which covers the emotions of the other race?" To Jefferson, white was beautiful. Even blacks themselves admitted so, he thought: "Add to these, flowing hair, a more elegant symmetry of form, their own judgment in favor of whites, declared by their preference of them, as uniformly as is the preference of Oranootan for the black woman over those of his own species." Given these differences, black removal was a way to preserve white qualities. Commenting on the breeding of domestic animals, Jefferson asked: "The circumstance of superior beauty is thought worthy of attention in the propagation of our horses, dogs, and other domestic animals; why not in that of man?" In his published book, *Notes on the State of Virginia*, Jefferson described the black population as a "blot" and insisted that the black, when freed, had to be removed "beyond the reach of mixture."[35]

Jefferson even devised a plan for black removal. To remove all of them at once, he thought, was not "practicable." He estimated that such a project would take twenty-five years, during which time the slave population would have doubled. Furthermore, the value of the slaves would amount to $600 million, and the cost of transportation and provisions would add up to $300 million. Jefferson recommended instead the deportation of the future generation of blacks; black infants would be taken from their mothers and trained in industrious occupations until they reached a proper age for deportation. Since Jefferson calculated a newborn infant was worth only $22.50, the estimated loss of slave property would be reduced from $600 million to only $37.5 million. Jefferson suggested they be transported to the independent black nation of Santo Domingo. "Suppose the whole annual increase to be sixty thousand effective births," he speculated on the future of blacks in America, "fifty vessels, of four hundred tons burthen each, constantly employed in that short run, would carry off the increase of every year, and the old stock would die off in the ordinary course of nature, lessening from the commencement until its final disappearance." He was confident the effects of his plan would be "blessed." As for the taking of children from their mothers, Jefferson remarked: "The separation of infants from their mothers . . . would produce some scruples of humanity. But this would be straining at a gnat, and swallowing a camel."[36]

In his discussion on Jefferson, Kohn neglects Jefferson's views on race and consequently fails to understand the founding father's ideas on American nationality. Likewise, in his analysis of the role of the educational system in the "integration" of the "products of many lands into a basic sense of 'belonging'," Kohn refers to Benjamin Rush's educational philosophy and Rush's desire to create a more "homogeneous" people, but ignores the Pennsylvania physician's attitudes toward blacks. To understand fully what Rush meant by a "homogeneous" American people, his essay on "Observations intended to favour a supposition that the black Color (as it is called) of the Negro is derived from the LEPROSY" cannot be overlooked. A signer of the Declaration of Independence, a seminal theoretician of American psychiatry, and one of the nation's leading educators, Dr. Rush read his essay at a meeting of the American Philosophical Society in 1792. In his "observations," he explained that a combination of factors—"unwholesome diet," "greater heat," "more savage manners," and "bilious fevers"—probably produced leprosy in the skin among blacks in Africa. Despite their condition of leprosy, blacks were as healthy and long-lived as whites, he claimed, for local diseases of the skin seldom affected general health or the duration of life. The more visible symptoms of leprosy were the Negro's physical features—the "big lip," "flat nose," "woolly hair," and especially the black color of his skin. A physician, Rush prescribed a "cure" for the sick Negro: "Depletion, whether by bleeding, purging, or abstinence has been often observed to lessen the black color in negroes. The effects of the above remedies in curing the common leprosy, satisfy me that they might be used with advantage in that state of leprosy which I conceive to exist in the skin of negroes." But until they could be "cured," Dr. Rush recommended an interim separation of the two races. "The facts and principles which have been delivered," he warned, "should teach white people the necessity of keeping up that prejudice against such connections with them (Negroes), as would tend to infect posterity with any portion of their disorder." To "cure" Negroes and to whiten the entire society would be, for Rush, to make the people of the new nation "more homogeneous."[37]

The third authority whom Glazer cites is Seymour Martin Lipset, author of *The First New Nation: The United States in Historical and Comparative Perspective.* According to Glazer, Lipset views the American Revolution as an event which weakened the ethnic identification with England and led to the emergence of equality and achievement as dominant values in American society. My own reading of Lipset suggests that he cannot be grouped with Arieli, Kohn, and Glazer himself. Where they tend to mix together ethnicity and race, Lipset makes a sharp distinction between the two: "American egalitarianism is, of course, for white men only. The treatment of the Negro makes a mockery of this value now as it has in the past."[38]

This perspective on an American "racial" pattern, while it is not developed or documented historically, leads Lipset to a very different conclusion than the one offered in Glazer's *Affirmative Discrimination.* Though both Lipset and Glazer share a similar understanding of American values, they separate on the issue of public policy and racial inequality. Where Glazer, from the perspective of the emergence of an American "ethnic" pattern, insists that all that can and should be done for blacks is to extend the legal status of equality to individuals regardless of race, Lipset contends that "perhaps the most important fact to recognize about the current situation of the American Negro is that *equality is not enough to assure his movement into the larger society.*" Where Glazer asserts that all the federal government should do is to outlaw racial discrimination in employment, Lipset points out the persistence of the enormous differentiation between white and black incomes, the disproportionate rate of unemployment among blacks, and the problems of structural black unemployment—the low level of education among blacks and the elimination of unskilled labor resulting from automation. "Fair employment legislation," Lipset argues, "does little good if there are no decent jobs available for which the bulk of Negroes are qualified. . . . To break this vicious cycle (of black illiteracy and unemployment), it is necessary to treat the Negro more than equally. . . ."[39]

But if Lipset is correct, how do we respond to what Glazer describes as "the remarkably rapid improvement in the black economic and occupational position in the 1960s"? If we look at certain kinds of data, we can find support for Glazer's contention that the "heritage of discrimination" can be eliminated by "simply attacking discrimination." As Glazer shows, in the North and West in 1969, the median income of black husband-wife families with family heads under 35 years of age was 91 percent of the median income of white families in the same category. For the nation as a whole, the median income of black husband-wife families rose from 62 percent of the median income of comparable white families in 1959 to 85 percent in 1972. During this period, blacks also made inroads into occupations of greater security and higher status. The percentage of male "Negroes and other races" (Glazer notes that this group as a whole is over 90 percent black) increased in several employment fields. Their percentages jumped from 4.9 percent in 1963 to 8.2 percent in 1973 for professional and technical workers, from 15.3 percent to 22.9 percent for white-collar workers, and from 10.7 percent to 14.9 percent for craft workers.[40]

But these advances, while important, must be analyzed within the total context of the black economic situation. While the black median income rose from 54 percent of the white median income in 1959 to 66 percent in 1969, it dropped back to 58 percent in 1972. Meanwhile, between 1959 and 1973, of all black families in poverty, those with male heads declined from 1,300,000 to 550,000, while families with female heads increased from 550,000 to 970,000. While black female-headed families constituted 23.7 percent of all black families in 1965, they increased to 34 percent in 1974, forming almost two-thirds of all black families in poverty. While blacks made important gains in several occupational fields, they remained behind whites. In 1973, only 8.2 percent of male "Negroes and other races" were professional and technical workers compared to 14.2 percent of whites, only 15.3 percent of them were white-collar workers compared to 41.7 percent of whites, and only 14.9 percent of them were craft workers compared to 21.5 percent of whites. While the unemployment rate for blacks and other races dropped from 12.6 percent (compared to 6.1 percent for whites) in 1958 to 6.7 percent (compared to 3.2 percent for whites) in 1968, it rose again to 9.9 percent (compared to 5.0 percent for whites) in 1974. Furthermore, while the unemployment rate for blacks and other races sixteen to nineteen years old dropped slightly from 27.4 percent (compared to 14.4 percent for whites) in 1958 to 25 percent (compared to 11.0 percent for whites) in 1968, it soared sharply to 32.9 percent (compared to 14.0 percent for whites) in 1974. Since the publication of Glazer's book in 1975, the median income of black families has continued to remain forty or more percentage points behind the median income of white families—43 percent in 1977 and 41 percent in 1978. The number of black single-parent families headed by women has also continued to rise, from 1.4 million in 1970 to 2.3 million in 1978, and has undercut much of the gains made by black two-spouse families which Glazer highlights. For every black family that made it into the middle class, three other black families joined the bottom of American society. While black families comprise 22 percent of all low-income households in 1970, they accounted for 28 percent in 1978.[41]

The total picture suggests the black economic situation is highly complex. We must acknowledge that some black "progress" has occurred. The number of blacks in the professional, technical, white-collar, and crafts occupations has increased. But we cannot claim this improvement was wholly the result of anti-discrimination legislation. We must also take into account the general expansion of the American economy in the 1960s as well as affirmative action pressures and policies which were in operation during this time of black economic improvement. Still, while recognizing these gains, we must not overlook or diminish the importance of the overriding and persistent reality of economic inequality between blacks and whites. Blacks still lag behind whites in median incomes, still find themselves underrepresented in the higher status and better-paying occupations, and still constitute a disproportionately large percentage of low-income and impoverished families. Moreover, underclass blacks may be facing a particularly grim future in a cybernated and service-producing economy. The high rate of black unemployment, which has been around twice the unemployment rate among whites, must be viewed within the context of a major structural shift from goods to service production; the proportion of workers in the service-producing sector of the economy has increased from 49 percent in 1947 to 64 percent in 1968. Thus employment expansion has been located largely in clerical, professional, and administrative fields, which have higher educational and training requirements for employment.[42]

What then is to be done and what would constitute responsible and informed public policies regarding the problem of racial inequality in America? How we answer this question will depend on how we perceive the problem—its nature and its history.

America, despite its racial pattern of domination and exclusion, contained a counterpointing perspective. In his resonant musings, a lonely poet—Walt Whitman—celebrated a vision of democratic tolerance and indiscriminate inclusionism. In Whitman's "America," peoples of all colors could come together, mixing in a great democracy yet respecting the rich cultural diversity of a multi-racial society. Thus the poet sang:

Of every hue and caste am I, of every rank and religion,
A farmer, mechanic, artist, gentleman, sailor, quaker,
Prisoner, fancy-man, rowdy, lawyer, physician, priest,
I resist any thing better than my own diversity.

Whitman saluted "all the inhabitants of the earth." For the American poet, "all races and cultures" were to be "accepted, to be saluted, not to be controlled or placed in hierarchy." And in America, all were to be welcomed—"Chinese, Irish, German, pauper or not, criminal or not— all, all, without exceptions." Ours was not to be a society for "special types" but for the "great mass of people—the vast, surging, hopeful army of workers."[43]

But Whitman's was not the vision of America's public policy makers. Where the poet offered a democratic alternative, the representatives to Congress enacted the 1790 Naturalization Law and the 1882 Chinese Exclusion Act. Where the poet joyfully perceived the promise of a culturally diverse America, federal officials removed Indians and relocated Japanese Americans. Where the poet embraced an egalitarianism for all, regardless of race, men in power like Jefferson, Rush, and Walker worked to build a homogeneous society for special types. Where the poet welcomed all immigrants into the "hopeful army of workers," corporate leaders like Crocker constructed racially divided segmented labor markets which reflected an American racial pattern.

This pattern was discerned long ago by Herman Melville and emblematized in his description of the crew of the Pequod and the whaling industry's labor force. "Not one in two of the many thousand men before the mast employed in the American whale fishery, are American born, though pretty nearly all the officers are," reported Melville's Ishmael. "Herein it is the same with the American whale fishery as with the American army and military and merchant navies, and the engineering forces employed in the construction of the American Canals and Railroads. The same, I say, because in all these cases the native American liberally provides the brains, the rest of the world as generally supplying the muscles." A significant supply of the "muscles" on board the Pequod had been drawn from workers of color—blacks, Indians, Pacific Islanders, and Asians. The social divisions within the ship's crew represented the occupational/racial structure in American labor and society. While not all whites were officers, all officers or men on deck were white, and all workers of color were below deck.[44]

The American racial pattern which Melville depicted in 1851 still exists today and will continue long after the enactment of legislation prohibiting discrimination based on color, race, or ethnic origin, unless public policies act affirmatively to overcome racial inequality. The problem of racial inequality is far more vexatious and profound than a simple matter of racial prejudice or an "American dilemma," and its solution will require far more than a mere prohibiton of racial discrimination. Due to racially exclusionist forces and developments in American history, racial inequality and occupational stratification coexist in a mutually reinforcing and dynamic structural relationship which continues to operate more powerfully than direct forms of racial prejudice and discrimination. Labor market segmentation, locating educated and skilled workers in the primary labor sector and uneducated and unskilled workers in the secondary labor market, perpetuates racial divisions in our society. In our cybernated and advanced industrial economy, universities contribute to this occupational/racial stratification; they train and certify students for entry into the professions or the "brain"-related sector of production. Thus universities, which continue to have disproportionate numbers of white students, help to reproduce a racially stratified social and employment structure in society.

Yet universities can become centers for challenging America's racial pattern. This mission can be especially important for publicly supported universities in states like California, where racial minorities constitute an increasing proportion of the taxpayers and where minority students continue to be proportionately underrepresented in enrollments at the University of California. As access institutions to the primary labor market, they can racially integrate their students to help assure greater employment opportunities for racial minorities. They can make certain qualified and trained minorities are available for professional and technical employment. As institutions of learning and research, universities can also promote cultural diversity in their curricula and generate a new body of critical scholarship. They can encourage a critical examination of American history and an imaginative formulation of new ideas and proposals for fundamental social changes. In this search for new knowledge and solutions, universities can become engaged in what Antonio Gramsci described as a "war for position on the cultural front"—informed, rigorous, and socially concerned intellectual activity to enable us to create a new critical vision, perhaps one in the tradition of Walt Whitman. Indeed, to rephrase historian Gabriel Kolko, we will not be able to choose alternatives to the racial pattern in America so long as none are seriously proposed.[45]

NOTES

[1] California State Department of Education Racial and Ethnic Survey (1977); *Report of the Joint Planning Committee,* The University of California: A Multi-Campus System in the 1980s (Berkeley: 1979); p. C 1; *University of California, Berkeley, Draft Long-Range Academic Plan Statement* (Berkeley: 1979), p. 20. Wisconsin, in terms of percentage of its

total population, will also have an increase in its racial minority population in the 1980s: In 1978 blacks, Hispanics, Native Americans, and Asians constituted 5.57 percent of the state's entire population; minority students comprised 6.7 percent of all 8th grade enrollments in public schools, indicating an increasing young minority population. See *Report of the University of Wisconsin System Committee to Review Minority Student Enrollment History and Projections, From Educational Access to Academic Success: A Design for Improving Opportunities for Minority Persons in Wisconsin Higher Education in the 1980s* (University of Wisconsin: February 1980), p. 18.

[2] Ronald T. Takaki, *Iron Cages: Race and Culture in 19th Century America* (New York: 1979); Nathan Glazer, *Affirmative Discrimination: Ethnic Inequality and Public Policy* (New York: 1978, originally published in 1975).

[3] For a critical review of the book, see Alexander Saxton, "Nathan Glazer, Daniel Moynihan and the Cult of Ethnicity: Review of *Affirmative Discrimination* by Nathan Glazer," in *Amerasia Journal* 4, No. 2 (1977): 141-500. See also Saxton, "Historical Explanations of Racial Inequality," in *Marxist Perspectives* 2, No. 2. (Summer 1979): 146-680. For other critical assessments of the "ethnic model," see Raymond S. Franklin and Solomon Resnik, *The Political Economy of Racism* (New York: 1973), especially pp. 132-83; *Robert Blauner, Racial Oppression in America* (New York: 1972), and Charles Valentine, *Culture and Poverty: Critique and Counterproposals* (Chicago: 1968).

[4] Glazer, *Affirmative Discrimination,* pp. ix, xvi, xvii.

[5] See ibid., chapters 2, 3, and 4.

[6] Ibid., pp. 220, 197, xi.

[7] Ibid., p. 194.

[8] Ibid., p. 204.

[9] Ibid., pp. 3, 4, 5.

[10] Ibid., p. 5.

[11] Ibid., pp. 5, 6, 7, 15, 17.

[12] Ibid., p. 5. Of course, the history of the last 200 years cannot be separated from the history of the preceeding 200 years, which have been studied by Winthrop Jordan in *White Over Black: American Attitudes Toward the Negro,* 1550-1812 (Chapel Hill: 1968). The significance of Jordan's work for our analysis is self-evident in its title.

[13] *Debates and Proceedings in the Congress of the United States,* 1789-1791, 2 vols. (Washington, D.C.: 1834), vol. 1: 998, 1284, vol. 2: 1148-56, 1162, 2264. For the Walter-McCarran Act, see Frank Chuman, *The Bamboo People: The Law and Japanese-Americans* (Del Mar, Calf.: 1976), p. 312. For a comprehensive discussion on citizenship, see James H. Kettner, *The Development of American Citizenship,* 1608-1870 (Chapel Hill: 1978), p. 14. Aaron H. Palmer, *Memoir,* geographical, political, and commercial, on the present state, productive resources, and capabilities for commerce, of Siberia, Manchuria, and the Asiatic Islands of the Northern Pacific Ocean; and on the importance of opening commercial intercourse with those countries, March 8, 1848. U. S. Cong., Senate, 30th Cong., 1st sess., Senate misc. no. 80, pp. 1, 52, 60, 61.

[15] Charles Crocker, testimony, in *Report of the Joint Special Committee to Investigate Chinese Immigration,* Senate Report No. 689, 44th Cong., 2nd sess., 1876-77, pp. 667, 679, 680.

[16] Chuman, *Bamboo People,* pp. 217, 218.

[17] Felix S. Cohen, *Handbook of Federal Indian Law* (Albuquerque: 1958, originally published in 1942), pp. 153-59.

[18] See Takaki, *Iron Cages*, p. 111.

[19] Francis Newton Thorpe, ed., *The Federal and State Constitutions, Colonial Charters, and Other Organic Laws of the States, Territories, and Colonies now or heretofore forming the United States of America* (Washington: 1909), vol. 1. *Treaty of Guadalupe-Hidalgo*, p. 381, *Constitution of California*, 1849, p. 393; Cohen, *Handbook of Federal Indian Law*, pp. 155-59.

[20] Glazer, *Affirmative Discrimination*, pp. 5, 22-29.

[21] "Statement of United States Citizenship of Japanese Ancestry," quoted in Michi Weglyn, *Years of Infamy: The Untold Story of America's Concentration Camps* (New York: 1976), p. 155.

[22] Cohen, *Handbook of Federal Indian Law*, p. 155.

[23] Andrew Jackson, "First Annual Message to Congress," in James D. Richardson, ed., *A Compilation of the Messages and Papers of the Presidents, 1789-1897* (Washington: 1897), 2: 456-58; Jackson to General John Coffee, April 7, 1832, in John Spencer Bassett, ed., *Correspondence of Andrew Jackson*, 6 vols. (Washington: 1926), 4: 430; Francis Amasa Walker, *The Indian Question* (Boston: 1874), pp. 10, 62-67.

[24] Francis Amasa Walker, *Annual Report of the Commissioner of Indian Affairs to the Secretary of the Interior for the Year 1872* (Washington: 1872), pp. 11, 63, 64, 77-79, 94, 95; *Indian Appropriation Act,* quoted in Walker, Indian Question, p. 5.

[25] For a discussion of the Dawes Act, see Takaki, *Iron Cages*, pp. 188-193.

[26] Glazer, *Affirmative Discrimination*, p. 8.

[27] Yehoshua Arieli, *Individualism and Nationalism in American Ideology* (Baltimore: 1966, originally published in 1964), p. 22; Glazer, *Affirmative Discrimination*, pp. 8-9.

[28] Glazer, *Affirmative Discrimination*, p. 12; Arieli, *Individualism and Nationalism*, p. 44; Benjamin Franklin, "Observations Concerning the Increase of Mankind" (1751), in Leonard W. Labaree, ed., *The Papers of Benjamin Franklin* (New Haven: 1959), 4: 234.

[29] Glazer, *Affirmative Discrimination*, p. 12; Alexis de Tocqueville, quoted in Arieli, *Individualism and Nationalism*, p. 17.

[30] Alexis de Tocqueville, *Democracy in America*, 2 vols. (New York: 1945, originally published in 1835), 1: 373-4, 352-3, 364.

[31] Ibid., pp. 370, 343-452.

[32] Hans Kohn, *American Nationalism: An Interpretative Essay* (New York: 1961, originally published in 1954), pp. 168, 139-175.

[33] Thomas Jefferson, quoted in Kohn, *American Nationalism*, requoted in Glazer, *Affirmative Discrimination*, p. 12; 34 "Jefferson to George Flower, September 12, 1817," in H. A. Washington, ed., *The Writings of Thomas Jefferson*, 7: 57-58.

[35] Thomas Jefferson, *Notes on the State of Virginia* (New York: 1964, originally published in 1785), pp. 85, 139, 133, 127; "Jefferson to Dr. Edward Bancroft, January 16, 1788," in Edwin M. Betts, ed., *Thomas Jefferson's Farm Book* (Princeton: 1953), p. 10.

[36] "Jefferson to Jared Sparks, February 4, 1824," in Paul L. Ford, ed., *The Works of Thomas Jefferson* (New York: 1892-99), 12: 334-39.

[37] Kohn, *American Nationalism,* pp. 173-74; Benjamin Rush, "Observations intended to favour a supposition that the black color (as it is called) of the Negroes is derived from the LEPROSY," *Transactions of the American Philosophical Society,* vol. 4. (1799): 289-97; Benjamin Rush, "Of the Mode of Education Proper in a Republic," in his *Essays, Literary, Moral & Philosophical* (Philadelphia: 1798), p. 19.

[38] Glazer, *Affirmative Discrimination,* p. 11; Seymour Martin Lipset, *The First New Nation: The United States in Historical and Comparative Perspective* (New York: 1967, originally published in 1963), pp. 379-80.

[39] Lipset, *First New Nation,* pp. 381-82.

[40] Glazer, *Affirmative Discrimination,* pp. 197-41-42.

[41] Ibid.; William J. Wilson, *The Declining Significance of Race: Blacks and Changing American Institutions* (Chicago: 1978), pp. 90, 91; *Current Population Reports,* Series P-20, Bureau of the Census, No. 340: "Household and Family Characteristics" (U.S. Government Printing Office: 1979), Table E, cited in Andrew Hacker, "Creating American Inequality," *New York Review of Books,* XXVII, No. 4: 23; see also ibid. for other comparisons. The most detailed study of this issue is Reynolds Farley, "Racial Progress in the Last Two Decades: What Can We Determine about Who Benefitted and Why?" paper presented at the 1979 Annual Meeting of the American Sociological Association.

[42] Dorothy K. Newman, et. al., *Protest, Politics, and Prosperity: Black Americans and White Institutions,* 1940-75 (New York: 1978), p. 64; Wilson, *Declining Significance of Race,* pp. 93-95.

[43] Walt Whitman, *Leaves of Grass and Selected Prose* (New York: 1958), pp. 38, 1, 25, 18, 78, 83, 89, 399-400, 340, 121, 343; Walt Whitman, in Horace Traubel, *With Walt Whitman in Canada,* 2 vols. (New York: 1915), 2: 34-35.

[44] Herman Melville, *Moby Dick, or the Whale* (Boston: 1956, originally published in 1851), pp. 108.

[45] For an introduction to Antonio Gramsci's ideas, see Gramsci, *The Modern Prince and Other Writings* (New York: 1972); also Gwynn Williams, "The Concept of 'Egemonia' in the Thought of Antonio Gramsci: Some Notes on Interpretation," *Journal of the History of Ideas* 21 (1960): 586-99; Eugene D. Genovese, "On Antonio Gramsci," in *In Red and Black: Marxian Explorations in Southern and Afro-American History* (New York: 1971), pp. 391-422. For the original statement from Gabriel Kolko, see Kolko, *The Triumph of Conservatism: A Reinterpretation of American History, 1900-1916* (New York: 1963), p. 304.

Government and the American Ethnic Pattern

Nathan Glazer

Harvard University

Our knowledge of public and governmental responses to race and ethnicity in the United States has exploded in the last fifteen years. It is odd that on an issue of such key and central importance in American life so much should have lain in darkness. But the attempt to establish equality, to expand the rights of ethnic and racial groups and to change their economic, social, political, and educational position, has led us into pathways and realms of inquiry that would otherwise never have been necessary. This is particularly the case in the United States because of the crucial role of law and of litigation to establish rights. Curiosity alone might never have led us into such arcane inquiries as when and how geographical boundary lines for elementary schools were set in cities, why some schools were expanded and others were not in the distant past, why new schools were sited where they were, why certain optional zones were established from which children could go to one or another school, why examination schools for the gifted were established and the nature of their admissions procedures over the years, and the like. We go into such research today because such recondite inquiries are necessary under law to demonstrate to a judge that unconstitutional segregation once existed or still exists in school districts that did not operate under state laws requiring segregation, or under local ordinances established on the basis of permissible state legislation.

Similarly, it is clear we are entering a period in which we will learn far more about the establishment of districts for purposes of representation in local elections than we ever found it necessary to know in the past. A simple history once told us that at-large elections or appointed commissions were once means to bring into government abler and more far-sighted representatives. This was the progressive version of the reason for the shift to at-large elections for city councils and school committees and for the replacement of election for commissions and boards by appointment. A later, more sophisticated theory pointed out that the progressive reformers had class interests as well as an interest in good government and wanted to exclude the less-educated immigrants, whom they thought of as not only less competent to conduct city government and education and more susceptible to corruption, but also more likely to tax the well-to-do more heavily. And so when the Irish began to elect mayors of Boston, it was arranged that the mayor of Boston should have less power; and when immigrants began to elect representatives from wards, it was arranged that elections become at-large so that prominent men supported by leading newspapers could overwhelm local ward candidates. Now we have yet another phase in the story, as the Department of Justice and varied litigants try to demonstrate that at-large voting was designed for or had the effect of depriving those groups protected by the Voting Rights Acts of 1965 and 1975 of their proper share of offices.

We are also learning far more about the history of employment and promotion and the use of tests to employ and promote, as a result of suits in the employment areas, than we ever knew before. And how could we ever have found out as much as we did about admissions procedures to medical schools, were it not for the great amount of confidential information revealed as a result of the legal action of Allan Bakke? We learned exactly what weight was put on tests, on grades, and just how far the admissions committee leaned in order to reach its quota of minority students.

And still another example: We know what exertions in historical research were attempted by the clerks to the Supreme Court Justices who had before them the key case of *Brown v. Board of Education.* Yet I think we would agree that Raoul Berger's further inquiries in *Government By Judiciary: The Transformation of the Fourteenth Amendment* (Harvard University Press, 1977) throw new light on what the framers of that amendment intended. His exertions were motivated not only by the pure desire to illuminate through history the meaning of key passages of the Constitution, a motivation that Berger had already fully demonstrated in his previous books on *Impeachment* and *Executive Privilege,* but also by the fact that contemporary developments had raised sharply the question of just what the Fourteenth Amendment meant, after all.

I would be the last to denigrate the enterprise and energy of historians exploring our past and our treatment of ethnic minorities and racial groups, but I think they would agree with me that the flood of information being made available by litigation in the effort to recast our present and future is throwing new light on our past.

What we know about the past is heavily determined by our intentions in the present. Presumably, different intentions would show (or bring to light) a somewhat different past. The intentions of today as expressed by the Department of Justice, the Office of Civil Rights of the Department of Education, the Equal Employment Opportunity Commission, the Civil Rights Commission, the National Association for the Advancement of Colored People, the varied public law groups that have sprung up to defend the rights of Mexican Americans, Puerto Ricans, Native Americans, Asians, and many other groups is to demonstrate a past of governmental oppression and segregation in order to justify a present and future of governmental preference. If schools in the past were zoned, sited, or regulated so as to separate white and black, then school attendance now must be so regulated that whites and blacks are distributed within them in proportion to their representation in the entire school district "Busing" has fortunately been devised as a simple one-word replacement for the description of the policy demanded by government and civil rights litigants that I have just offered. If the pattern of geographical representation in the past was devised for, or had the effect of, maximizing the power of one group, then it may be dismantled or changed to maximize the power of the deprived group. If promotions and testing were devised to exclude one group, or had the effect of excluding a group, they may be changed to require a fixed proportion of that excluded group—and so on. Thus the past is reshaped by the needs of the present.

I have spoken of legal needs. Of course the defense of existing practices also requires a resort to history, sometimes with greater and sometimes with fewer resources to burrow into the past than litigants on the offensive can afford. But the terms of the examination are set by the plaintiffs.

These terms are also determined by the interests and capacities of those capable of doing the digging—historians, sociologists, political scientists, academics in the social sciences generally—working along with lawyers to develop cases that led to findings of discrimination and segregation. It needs no deep examination to reveal that the qualified researchers are on the whole men of liberal and even radical inclination. Whatever the circumstances in the past—when historians and sociologists, as we are told by Oscar Handlin and others, believed in the significance of race for individual behavior and the future of the nation and argued for immigration restriction and segregation—we would all agree the situation today is radically different. Sociologists are among the most liberal of academics, and academics are among the most liberal of occupational groups of Americans, certainly when it comes to questions of race.

Finally, the terms of the examination are set by the general intellectual climate. Who is interested in defending these days—I now speak
of writers, reporters, commentators, as well as professional scholars—
the United States as an exemplar of democracy and equality? The
American celebration is far behind us; its heyday was in the 1950s, in
the afterglow of a successful war against the chief apostle of racism,
when America seemed to most of its intellectual elite to be good as well
as powerful. I do not know in what order that reputation was lost, but
America is now seen by its intellectual elite as neither good nor powerful. Not only is it believed to uniformly support undemocratic, dictato-
rial, and inhuman regimes, but it is no longer seen as a good home for
those who come here from poorer countries or by its intellectuals and
commentators as a place where poor people may raise themselves
through their own efforts. Indeed, this viewpoint may be so. The
present perception, however, shapes our view of the past, and while the
flood of books and studies of the later 1960s and 1970s demonstrating
the unrelieved racism of the American past has somewhat abated, we
now have the scholarly demonstration that the past was indeed so.

Ronald Takaki presents such a scholarly version of our past. It is
based on solid research, research which has taken him behind quota-
tions I (and others) have used to argue a different view of the American past, and one which permits him to present an almost unrelieved
picture of a racist America. Our treatment of race, he argues, has been
different from our treatment of white ethnic groups. For the latter, he
grants it may be true that the United States was an open country and
that through most of its history it permitted them to enter freely, offered them economic opportunity, allowed them to become citizens,
and gave them the freedom to retain as much of their culture, language, and religion as they wished. But the experience of groups of
non-white races was radically different, and all the points above are
simply not true for them. They were not allowed free entry, they were
not offered economic opportunity, they were not allowed to become
citizens, they were not allowed to retain their cultures. For persons of
races other than white, the United States was not a land of freedom—
it was a racist and oppressive society.

Nor has anything changed in recent years. As Takaki writes, "The
American racial pattern which Melville depicted in 1851 still exists
today and will continue long after the enactment of legislation prohibiting discrimination based on color, race, or ethnic origin, unless public
policies act affirmatively to overcome racial inequality." When I, in
Affirmative Discrimination, described the emerging American ethnic
pattern (the chapter in which I did so was titled "The Emergence of an
American Ethnic Pattern"), a description Takaki has taken as his

text, I added, "There is of course a breathtaking arrogance in asserting that *this* has been *the* course of American history." I followed with a page pointing to the well-known history—a history developed in much more elaborate detail in Takaki's essay—which points the other way, to defend the thesis that the course of American history has been and remains racist. I will not rehearse all these facts. The question raised in my chapter, however, was what is the *direction* of American history? Where is it going? Toward the further and continued exclusion of men and women of other races? In the direction of denying them the suffrage and full rights of citizenship? In the direction of preventing their social, economic, and political rise? In the direction of restricting their right to exercise and expand their culture and language?

It is in the light of these questions that I find Takaki's assertion that the relations between the races in this country of 1851 still survive and will survive unless undescribed policies take place far more breathtaking than my attempt to discern the direction American society was taking in the treatment of race and ethnicity. Not only does Takaki homogenize the entire past in a way which is unrecognizable, the past is homogenized with the present in a way which is unrecognizable.

Consider two examples of this homogenization of the past. Takaki argues that between the Naturalization Law of 1790 and the McCarran Act of 1952, no non-white could become a citizen. This is a radical simplification of a complex situation. The fact is that black immigrants could and did become naturalized long before the McCarran Act as a result of Congressional action in 1870, that many Asians were also naturalized in the nineteenth and early twentieth centuries despite this formal ban, but perhaps more significantly, naturalization and citizenship were of no major consequence in limiting or affecting peoples's rights for a good part of the nineteenth century.[1] What I asserted in describing the emerging American ethnic pattern and the decisions taken over a period of time that defined it was that "the entire world would be allowed to enter the United States." This was American policy until 1882. Restriction was then imposed on Chinese—later and in a more limited degree on Japanese—and extended in the first Quota Act of 1921 to all persons outside the Americas, with a specific impact on Southern and Eastern Europeans; this was modified slightly in 1944, more extensively in 1952, and abandoned in 1965. Today most immigration into the United Staes is from Asia and Latin America and consists of just those peoples whom, according to Takaki, a racist society keeps down—and out. How then does one explain the fact that during 1971-77, only 20.4 percent of immigrants were from Europe, while 31.7 percent were from Asia and 45.4 percent from the Americas—almost all from Latin America, and much of which undoubtedly carries some racial admixture, either black or Native American?[2] Certainly if one wants to make an argument against this first point of the emerging American ethnic pattern—that our policy has been to make the right of entry ever more inclusive in racial and ethnic terms until, as I wrote, "the entire world would be allowed to enter the United States"—one cannot ignore the character of the stream of immigration to the United States for the past fifteen years.

A second example of the homogenization of history, so that all of it is reduced to one smooth record of racism: Takaki describes quite accurately how blacks were denied the vote in the past, even in the North. He leaps from the New York Constitution of 1821, the Pennsylvania Constitution of 1838, and the systematic exclusion of blacks from the vote in the South after the Civil War to the Voting Rights Act of 1965, and writes: "Thus the 1965 law, enacted in response to massive black pressure and protest under the leadership of Martin Luther King, was a break from a long history of denial of voting rights to racial as opposed to 'ethnic' minority citizens." What is ignored and elided in this history is the entire record of black participation in voting and politics in the *North*. This record was evident to anyone growing up in New York in the 1930s and 1940s. Nor was New York City (or state) exceptional. "In the North," Gunnar Myrdal wrote in 1944, on the basis of his researches in the late 1930s and early 1940s, "Negroes have the vote like other people and there is nowhere a significant attempt to deprive them of the franchise."[3] Takaki writes as if the 1965 act was necessary to get the vote for blacks in the United States generally, and speaks of it as a "break" rather than the culmination of the process of gaining for blacks exactly the same rights as exist for whites.

All this is not to deny that Tocqueville was an accurate observer of American racism in the North and South, or that Benjamin Franklin and Thomas Jefferson were unwilling to see this nation become as diverse as its founding principles promised it might become—and that in fact it did become. It is not to deny that one can tell a grim story of American racism, directed against American Indians, blacks, Mexicans and other Latin Americans, Asians, and others. But then a number of other questions arise which are not treated by Takaki but which it seems to me are essential if we are to analyze American ethnic and racial policy today.

One is a question of basically historical interest: What was the weight of these racist beliefs, practices, and policies in affecting the development of the United States as an ethnically diverse society? It turns out that they did not prevent the greatest migration in the world. Nor did the groups we discriminated against stay out. Insofar as conditions in this country offered greater opportunities and more freedom than conditions in their home countries, people flowed into the United States until the doors began to close to certain groups in the 1880s and to most in the 1920s; and they still flow in, predominantly from Asia and Latin America since immigration policy was stripped of its racial and ethnic preferences in the 1960s.

A second question of some importance arises: To what extent can we draw sharp lines in American policy differentiating ethnic from racial groups, such that ethnic groups were full candidates for inclusion into American society and non-white racial groups were not and are not? I think the significance of this line is greatly exaggerated.[4] Jews, Italians and Greeks were considered in the early twentieth century racially different from whites by leading American scholars. Their characterization as racially different changed under the impact of both their changing social and economic position and of the general disrepute into which racist thinking fell in the 1930s and 1940s. Chinese and Japanese, despite the fierce prejudice and discriminatory laws to which they were subjected, and despite the discriminatory treatment of Japanese in World War II, today suffer no clearly definable handicap because of race. They get as much or more education, enter as prestigious or more prestigious occupations, are as active in politics as white Americans—and by the measures of education, occupation, and political activity and success, may be doing better than a number of European ethnic groups. There is some evidence that their income does not match their occupations. It would be very difficult to ascribe this to discrimination; living in this society and observing it, I have the impression the discrimination against Asians is as fragmentary and minor as the discrimination against Jews. The position of the Chinese and Japanese has changed radically as a result of their own economic and social mobility, a strong turn against and decline in racist attitudes and policies that we can date from World War II and which has been continuous and steady, and the rise of a policy of nondiscrimination which has no exceptions in law and which I believe is generally effective in practice.

Hispanic Americans raise a problem for the theory of the sharp line between ethnicity and race as determining factors in American racial and ethnic policy. Are they to be considered ethnic, racial, or divided between the two categories? Cubans have shown substantial economic and social mobility. Their experience does not seem markedly different from that of moderately successful European immigrants. Latin Americans from Colombia, Nicaragua, and other countries now providing legal and illegal immigrants also seem to be experiencing the same strains and the same hope of mobility through hard work and education that characterized European immigrants in the past. Mexicans have been subjected to much discrimination in the past. Today their problems stem from poor education and a background in a poor and traditional society which provides them with inadequate skills for success in the United States, rather than from discrimination. The middle-class Mexican does not face discrimination. The Puerto Ricans are the worst off—and yet is it discrimination that explains their poor economic position? I would think other causes are more immediate and more effective. They have done badly in the public schools of their chief port of entry—worse than other immigrants have done in these schools in the past or do in them in the present—perhaps because of the stronghold of Spanish created by the close contact with Puerto Rico, perhaps because of those obscure familial and social background factors that we know lead to differential success of ethnic groups in education. They have come from a poor island to a city presently becoming poor and rapidly losing the jobs immigrants might take. They have entered a city and area in which welfare was well-developed—and have become the group that proportionately makes greatest use of it. Certainly if European ethnic groups had entered an America in which one could do better on welfare, in terms of income and services, than poor-paying jobs could offer, the impact on participation in the labor force would also have been substantial. In any case, the very different experiences of groups of Hispanic background suggest that the lumping of all of these as a group requiring special protection from discrimination (along with, oddly enough, Spanish immigrants and their descendants—but not Portuguese) is a radical oversimplification.

Another group which is included on the racial side of the ethnic-racial distinction to make the case that non-white races are treated differently from white ethnic groups are Native Americans. Once again, I accept all the details of Takaki's indictment. One must add, of course, that the United States, as the colonies before them, were often in a state of war with Indian tribes, and there was great savagery on both sides, more justifiable in the case of Stone Age peoples than that of presumably advanced Europeans. But the situation of Indians was radically different from that of enslaved or free blacks, Asian laborers, and other groups with which they are grouped in the amalgam of "race." They were the indigenous inhabitants, and in a process which morality cannot justify but which has occurred whenever peoples of radically different levels of technical accomplishment meet—whether on the island of Hokkaido or the southern tip of Africa—were driven off lands which Europeans wanted and confined to reservations. But the point I want to make is that it was inevitable their status should be ambiguous. They were not considered—nor did they consider themselves—as candidates for full participation in an evolving nation. For many years now they have had the opportunity to take the same position any other American citizen has, or to retain tribal status with its various rights and privileges. What is owed them now is complex—legally, morally, and politically. They remain the only ethnic or racial group that is given a distinct definition and status in American law. But this is for their protection, not oppression. To describe their situation today in terms of racist oppression is to take a complex history, in which racist oppression in the past played a substantial role, and to reduce it to a caricature. The question of the fate and future of Native Americans today depends today on them, not on how other Americans treat them. They can enter the polity freely with all the rights and duties of any other American or maintain tribal status, which to many is more desirable because it offers the opportunity of maintaining a distinctive culture, as well as the benefits in federal aid that now flow to the organized tribes.

Blacks remain the one example that defends almost without modification the argument that whites and European ethnic groups have been treated radically differently from non-white races. If the argument were that blacks were treated radically differently from whites, there could be no counter-argument. They were enslaved, a great body of law was developed to keep them in subjection, and the effort to raise them to something like equal status in various respects after the Civil War failed. What I object to is the taking of the distinctive and tragic history of black Americans and generalizing it into a distinctive American racist tradition affecting all non-white groups in the past and the present. The treatment of groups in American societies rather suggests a continuum in which some were clearly favored and entered mainstream American society with the most minimal difficulties, while others faced various degrees of prejudice and exclusion—degrees determined by language, religion, culture, and yes, among others, racial difference. But just as the experience of European white ethnic groups shows great differences among them, so do the experiences of groups defined by different race.

But now a third question: whatever the fate of the argument over the degree of prejudice, discrimination and exclusion faced by groups in the past, what is the relevance of this past to the situation we face today? One element of relevance is clear: the past affects what people become in complex ways. The prejudice and discrimination faced by Jews and Japanese may have contributed to their greater efforts and success in acquiring education; the prejudice and discrimination faced by blacks and Mexican Americans may have had the opposite consequences. Is the past relevant, however, to policies today that are designed to give a special preference and protection to a number of groups, specifically blacks, Native Americans, Hispanics and Asians, with the latter two in particular being agglomerations with indistinct boundaries? I do not want at this point to prejudge this question but only to make the point that a concentration on the oppression of the past, with a total silence over the shift to a policy of preference today, is a clear implicit argument that only the past is relevant. In Takaki's case, it goes further—to the implication that the past is still with us not only in its heritage but even in its policies, except for inconsequential changes. That is, to quote again, "The American racial pattern that Melville depicted in 1851 is still with us. . . ." In contrast, I do not believe the facts of present preference can be denied, though there are many other things that may be argued about it, such as its scale, extent, effectiveness, and justice. It is in connection with justice that I assume Takaki emphasizes in such rich detail the indignities of the past, for, as in a legal brief, the injustice of the past may give a claim to redress in the present; and Takaki's essay indeed, with all its richness of historical reference, reads like such a brief. In the law affecting civil rights as it has developed, it turns out it does not matter if an act that demands redress took place in 1954 or in 1980—indeed the record in school desegregation cases is often extended back into the nineteenth century. But in life, it does matter what happens today and in the near yesterday, as well as in the distant past. It is one thing to establish what the facts were. It is another to insist that the facts of the past, no matter how distant the past, have an undiluted relevance for what we do today. From the point of view of government's present role in race and ethnicity, it is hard for me to see much relevance to the story Takaki has told. Far more relevant are the policies of today, and it is to these and some characterization of them that I will devote the rest of this essay.

In effect, government's role has shifted from an ideal of color-blindness—an ideal carefully specified in the Civil Rights Act of 1964—to a practice of color consciousness, as realized in the practice of affirmative action in employment, busing and requirements for bilingual education in elementary and secondary education, and direct federal efforts to maximize the voting of certain specified racial and language groups. A full outline of all these policies is beyond the scope of this essay. I have described some of them elsewhere. But to review the situation briefly:

Employment

Both public and non-public employers now come under the provisions of Title VII of the Civil Rights Act, which prohibits discrimination on grounds of race, color, religion, sex, or national origin, and which is enforced by the Equal Employment Opportunity Commission. This agency, with now 4,000 employees and a budget of $125 million, responds to individual complaints of discrimination. More important, it decides what discrimination is. In this role, for example, tests in which the ethnic and racial groups, defined by the EEOC as being in particular need of protection, score more poorly than others, are suspect of being discriminatory devices and subject to severe limitations in their use. The Commission also takes the position that the employees of any major employer should mirror the population, and that if it does not, the employer may be guilty of discrimination. As important as the EEOC is the Office of Federal Contract Compliance Programs in the Department of Labor, with 1,450 employees and a budget of $53 million, which oversees compliance with an executive order that requires "affirmative action"—now defined as achieving an employee mix in which the specially protected groups are represented according to their "availability" in the population—of government contractors, who include all major employers and apparently all college and universities and hospitals, because of their dependence (or their students' or patients' dependence) on federal funds. Basically, all employers in the country, except for the smallest and for religious organizations, must be concerned over whether their employees represent properly the population at large—or rather, more specifically, those groups that are the particular concern of the EEOC and the OFCCP.[5]

Education

The major thrust of federal policy in the field of elementary and secondary education, stemming from the historic Supreme Court decision of 1954 outlawing segregation, has been to achieve a racial mix in each school representative of the distribution in each district, and where this results in black and other minority children becoming a majority in a school, federal policy is aiming at combining districts so that blacks and other minority children may be a minority in each school. This policy is carried forward primarily by the federal courts (owing to the opposition to busing—the only means by which this policy can be carried out—in Congress) and by the Department of Justice. The legal bases for these policies are now almost complete. In 1979 the Supreme

Court ruled in the Dayton and Columbus cases that some degree of segregation in 1954—when the Brown decision occurred—was a sufficient legal basis for finding a school district in violation of the Constitution today and would trigger the busing solution. Under this decision busing could be required in every city in the country.[6] More recently the Department of Justice has launched a full-scale effort to bring together Houston and its suburbs so that a district could be created in which black and Hispanic children might be, for a time, in a minority.[7] Whether the policy of elimination of schools with high black concentration is to be considered a matter of preference is another matter. Many black parents oppose busing, as do most white. Nevertheless, this is the major thrust of policy today.

A second major effort in the elementary and secondary schools, in this case carried forward by the Office of Civil Rights of the Department of Education, is to require some degree of bilingual education in all school districts with minimal numbers of children of foreign language background. The major beneficiaries of this policy—if indeed it is to be considered a benefit—are Spanish-speaking children, or at least children who come from Spanish-speaking homes. The Office of Civil Rights operates under the authority of its own regulations, as given minimal but adequate support by the Supreme Court in the *Lau* decision. There are arguments over what kind of education should be provided, but in many cases under court order or OCR pressure, it is a full education in key subjects in Spanish for a number of years. There is also considerable dispute over how long education in a foreign language should continue.[8]

Once again, whether this should be called "preference" is an arguable matter. Perhaps children of foreign language background would more rapidly learn English, progress in school, and achieve a higher level of performance under a policy which simply taught them English through immersion as rapidly as possible. This was the path earlier immigrants took (or were forced to take), insofar as they did not establish private schools in their own language, and one suspects this is the path most Asian immigrants—Korean, Vietnamese, Filipino, Chinese—prefer today. But it is at any rate a policy which, in direct contrast to the assimilating policies of the past, responds to the demands and concerns of at least some part of the leadership of some ethnic groups. This policy is also implemented for the most part by Hispanics staffing the relevant federal agencies—just as agencies implementing affirmative action in employment show a preponderance of blacks.

Finally, in higher education, policies have developed independently of the federal government which serve to increase overall minority enrollment, particularly in the selective professional schools for law and medicine. These policies have also been dubbed with the term "affirm-ative action," which might be more narrowly limited to the employ-ment policies that have been developed under the authority of the "af-firmative action" requirement of the executive order governing federal contractors. They have been given wide publicity by the DeFunis and Bakke cases, and despite an ambiguous and complex decision by the Supreme Court which bans quotas in their crudest forms, are still con-tinued under another part of the Supreme Court decision in Bakke which allows the taking of race into consideration.[9]

Voting

Finally, in this brief round-up of the present state of policy, it is neces-sary to refer to the federal government's effort to maximize the voting power of blacks and some other groups under the Voting Rights Act of 1965 and its revision in 1975 to cover specified language groups.

While this act is intended to eliminate discrimination against some groups in voting, it contains provisions which require local jurisdic-tions to provide voting materials in various foreign languages and reg-ulates the imposition of requirements for voting by states and local jurisdictions. Under the act the Department of Justice has redrawn congressional and other districts to increase minority representation.[10]

There is much, much more that might and should be said about these and other policies, but I wish to avoid excessive detail to raise some key questions about these policies in general. These policies can be characterized as breaking with a consensus that was built painfully in this country over seventy years from *Plessy v. Ferguson,* which le-gitimated the segregation of blacks, to the Civil Rights Act of 1964, which declared separate treatment in many areas on grounds of race, color, or national origin to be illegal. The consensus was built through action in the federal courts by organized civil rights groups, which in-cluded black and white, by legislation in the progressive Northern states, by presidential initiatives, and finally by massive congressional action, and it was supported overwhelmingly by the American people by the mid-1960s. America was trying to become a society in which no man or woman's race or ethnicity would affect that person's fate, be-cause government and key nongovernmental agencies would be re-quired to operate under a cloak of ignorance as to any individual's race or ethnic background. The cloak of ignorance went so far that under some laws it was illegal to require a picture from an applicant to a college or university.

The cloak of ignorance has now been lifted, with some reluctance from Congress, primarily by action of executive agencies that enforce nondiscrimination and affirmative action requirements supported by the federal courts. The lifting of the cloak of ignorance means that every individual's race and ethnic background becomes a key datum for an employer, for a school, college, or university, for the federal enforcing agencies, for local voting registrars. The larger questions raised are whether these actions are necessary to defend the rights of protected groups or whether in imposing these requirements we are throwing away the possibility of a color-blind society—one in which government and major institutions treat each individual as an individual, and race, ethnic background and language are a matter for the individual and his group to take account of in any way he wishes.

As to whether these actions are necessary depends on how one views the degree of active discrimination that exists in this country today, and whether one is convinced that acts of discrimination will be so widespread and so devious that only a statistical determination of whether discrimination has occurred or is occurring is possible. If one can demonstrate discrimination only through statistics, the recording of race and ethnicity is necessary in order to have the statistics to make a case; and more significantly, the remedy that will be imposed will be a statistical one also. Persons will be hired or promoted or admitted according to whether they fulfill a statistical goal or quota. Thus we will need to know a person's race and ethnic background both to determine discrimination and implement a remedy. This is the way we are now going. Hiring by goals is widespread among government contractors and in government, and hiring by quota is imposed in consent judgments on many police and fire departments and private employers as a result of cases charging discrimination. The accused parties accept these judgments to hire by quota because the pattern of court decisions makes statistical evidence demonstrating discrimination easy to bring forward and hard to refute. A report on a major case brought by the Department of Labor against the Harris Trust & Savings Bank charging discrimination demonstrates the present posture:

> Precedent-setting statistical analyses, based on the bank's computerized personnel files, were offered as evidence by both sides. The bank's statistical work consumes four volumes, for example. Human witness played a rather minor role. Only 14 present or former bank employees were called by the litigants to testify to either discrimination or equal treatment. No one even suggested that these witnesses were representative of present and former bank employees.

John L. Stephens, head of employee relations at Harris Bank, is quoted as saying: "I think the whole process is going to become quotas. The Government is going to apply quotas and you're going to have to meet them. Good-faith efforts towards goals aren't sufficient. The government will mandate management systems and tell corporations how to manage their personnel systems. They're usurping management."[11] Mr. Stephens is more aggressive and forthright than most other personnel managers. Most accept consent decrees specifying what proportion of each group must be hired or promoted at each level, as did A.T. & T. some years ago.

Whether or not necessary to end discrimination, are these measures necessary to improve the economic position of depressed minorities and, in particular, blacks? Clearly some minorities, including racial minorities, advance without quotas. Quotas will lead to increased numbers being hired and promoted. But employers, governmental and private, are also interested in efficiency. The best black—or other minority—employees are advanced. In some cases, one will find employers bidding for the services of the relatively few blacks who have the qualifications for certain jobs, leading to the bidding up of their salaries and their rapid movement from one job to another. Whether this kind of governmental intervention will do much for the fate of the group in general is still an open question. It is still an interesting fact that blacks fared better and progressed more rapidly in the later 1960s, in the wake of the Civil Rights Act but before affirmative action was widely implemented in 1970 and 1971, than they have since, while affirmative action has become a norm in American employment and while the agencies enforcing it have grown enormously. Clearly the growing economy of the 1960s did more for blacks than the regime of government enforcement in an era of slowing growth in the 1970s. Just what affirmative action has done for the major target group, blacks, is still an open question.[12]

In any case, the sober reality is that massive government programs of public and subsidized employment and employment training and of enforcement of nondiscrimination and affirmative action have made little inroads on the massive problem of unemployed and underemployed black youth, whatever they may have done to improve the conditions of the qualified, aspiring, and upwardly mobile. Clearly one can envisage—though not in the current political circumstances—even more massive efforts, such as simple quota requirements given all employers. But one might in that case fear that the loss of efficiency could contribute further to the relative decline of the American economy in the face of efficient foreign competition, to the detriment of all groups, including the protected minorities.

These are clearly only speculations on the effect of affirmative action—and possibly stronger future affirmative action—on the fate of those among the protected groups that now score well below average standards in income and in representation in prestige occupations. More research is needed, though a great deal has already been brought forth by the litigational environment I described at the beginning of this essay. And now that we have public law groups defending accused parties as well as acting for plaintiffs, even more such research will be generated.

It is possible that nothing will do as much as fast to raise the economic position of the most backward of the protected groups—blacks and Puerto Ricans—as strongly enforced affirmative action, despite my doubts. We then come to the largest question raised by the new policy, and that is: What are the costs of giving up the color-blind policy and color-blind ideal for a color-conscious policy? I am not sure anyone argues for a color-conscious ideal, that is, a society monitored so that each of certain defined racial and ethnic groups will be guaranteed some given proportions of admissions to selective professional schools, of lawyers and doctors, of managers and government employees, of skilled workers, and other occupational categories—with action required when a group falls below the average. No one has worked out how such a society could be run, though we are being given some interesting examples from abroad, as in Belgium. I would argue to begin with that color-conscious policies will become the ideal—a tarnished ideal, perhaps, but one held up by government enforcement agencies and defended by representatives of the protected groups. The policy will become an ideal because it will become permanent, and a permanent policy presented as the answer to an age-old record of discrimination must become an ideal. When through policy means the EEOC is satisfied with the employment pattern of minority groups at Sears, GM, and other major companies, there will be no way of giving up the goals and quotas. When the supervision formally ends because the corporation has hired and promoted the numbers EEOC and OFCCP require, will there then not be continued monitoring necessary to make sure the numbers are kept up? And at that point, after massive changes have occurred in personnel systems, with most tests banned, with hiring increasingly dictated by race and ethnicity, how will we get back to systems that take the individual as the standard regardless of group? Politically and socially, withdrawal from a fully developed system in which admissions, employment and promotions are dominated by race and ethnic categories is very hard to envisage.

And what will have been lost? It will depend on one's values whether anything has been lost. If one's values are individualist, if one truly feels that race and ethnicity and color should not govern an individual's fate, much will have been lost when a great experiment in creating a multi-ethnic society dominated by individualist values comes to an end. Like other countries that struggle with the problems of an ethnically pluralist population, we would have given up and decided we simply have to share out the goods by the numbers, so much for each group. Older Americans, who were raised fighting for a different objective, will feel the loss more than younger Americans, who have already lived for ten years with such a regime—and will live with it for many years. The argument made many years ago by Thurgood Marshall in his brief in *Sipuel* will then sound odd: as he said there, "Classifications and distinctions based on race and color have no moral or legal validity in our society."[13] Of course he was then speaking of classifications and distinctions made to keep people down. But he spoke with such directness because he never dreamed that thirty years later they would have been replaced with classifications and distinctions to raise people up. Legally, the revolution is almost complete, though there are still a few details for the Supreme Court to settle. Morally, there is still substantial objection to the notion that this is right. Politically, the force to reverse this revolution, carried through by federal agencies and federal judges, supported by the better educated and the molders of opinion, has not yet been and I doubt really can be mustered. What kind of society it will create we will wait and see.

NOTES

[1] I draw these points from an excellent review of naturalization and citizenship policy, "Citizenship, Naturalization, and Aliens" by Reed Ueda, in the *Harvard Encyclopedia of American Ethnic Groups.*

[2] *Statistical Abstract of the United States, 1978,* p. 88.

[3] Gunnar Myrdal, *An American Dilemma* (New York: Harper and Row, 1944), p. 437.

[4] Nathan Glazer, "Blacks and Ethnic Groups: The Difference, and the Political Difference it Makes," in *Key Issues in the Afro-American Experience,* ed. Nathan I. Huggins, Martin Kilson, and Daniel M. Fox (New York: Harcourt Brace Jovanovich, 1971), II: 193-211.

[5] For further details, see Nathan Glazer, *Affirmative Discrimination,* (Basic Books), Ch. 2; and Nathan Glazer, "Affirmative Discrimination: Where Is It Going?", *International Journal of Comparative Sociology* XX (March-June 1979): 1-2. The literature on this subject is voluminous, and for the latest details one must resort to law reports. For additional material on the complex question of "availability" and the issues that have arisen between government and employers on how it is to be determined, see *Perspectives on Availability* (Washington, D.C.: Equal Employment Advisory Council, 1978).

[6] *Columbus Board of Education v. Penick,* 99 S.Ct. 2941 (1979), and *Dayton Board of Education v. Brinkman,* 99 S.Ct. 2971 (1979).

[7] Department of Justice news release, May 15, 1980.

[8] For an account of the rise of this policy, see Nathan Glazer, "Public Education and American Pluralism," *Parents, Teachers, and Children* (San Francisco: Institute for Contemporary Studies, 1977). For a current analysis, see Abigail M. Thernstrom, "Congress and Bilingual Education: A Flawed Performance," *The Public Interest,* Summer 1980.

[9] See for a review of this issue, Allan P. Sindler, *Bakke, DeFunis, and Minority Admissions* (New York: Longman, 1978).

[10] See Abigail M. Thernstrom, "The Odd Evolution of the Voting Rights Act," *The Public Interest,* Spring 1979.

[11] Bill Barnhart, "Statisticians enter the battle in U.S. regulation cases," *Chicago Tribune,* December 5, 1979.

[12] For some data on this, see Glazer, *Affirmative Discrimination,* pp. 21-23, and references there.

[13] Terry Eastland and William J. Bennett, *Counting by Race* (New York: Basic Books, 1979), p. 98.

The Science and Politics of Ethnic Enumeration[1]

Ira S. Lowry

The Rand Corporation, Santa Monica, California

Introduction

In April 1979, the Bureau of the Census began its decennial effort to detail the ethnic composition of the American population. Its conclusions will be of much more than academic interest; under current laws and regulations, the 1980 census reports on ethnicity will significantly influence everyone's access to education, employment, housing, and a wide assortment of federal benefits. It is therefore important for us as citizens as well as scientists to understand and assess the Bureau's plans for ethnic enumeration.

Unfortunately, the Bureau does not know how to conduct a scientific ethnic census. That should not be surprising, because social science has yet to offer validated methodological instruction. In fact, I see the elements of a vicious circle. Most scientific research dealing with ethnic distinctions relies on census data and therefore on the ethnic concepts used in past censuses. The main plea of the science lobby is for continuity in census concepts and methods, so the Bureau is encouraged to perpetuate its follies. Only rarely do social scientists challenge the absence of a coherent conceptual basis for the Bureau's ethnic distinctions, or the known unreliability of the methods it uses to identify an individual's ethnic status. Those who do challenge are ineffective because they cannot offer better alternatives.

Where science is weak, politics flourish. Civil rights legislation since 1960 has created vested interests in ethnic classification and enumeration, interests whose efforts are clearly visible in the 1980 census instrument and field procedures. Various ethnic lobbies have pressed hard for separate status in census reporting, for more complete enumeration of their constituencies, and for identification procedures that classify marginal cases with a favored group. Ethnic enumeration has become so important a practical issue that the federal Office of

Management and Budget has imposed a uniform system of ethnic accounting on all federal agencies, including the Bureau of the Census.

In my judgment, the Bureau has dealt responsibly with all these pressures, embracing the most sensible and resisting the most outrageous proposals. But this balancing act will become increasingly difficult if, as I expect, ethnic lobbies multiply and their influence increases. The Bureau badly needs a solidly scientific basis for ethnic concepts and enumeration procedures as a defense against manipulation. This essay concludes by recommending some specific steps the Bureau could take toward securing the knowledge it needs.

The Concept of Ethnicity

Throughout this essay, I shall use the term "ethnicity" to denote a particular kind of social identity—that which derives from belonging to a group whose members share a common race, religion, language, or national origin, or some combination of these factors.[2] Such groups are larger than families and, usually, smaller than nations; and the members of each are bound together by their sense of a common history and destiny, often despite powerful differences in values and life styles.

Because ours is a nation of immigrants formed in an era of global upheaval and long-distance migration, we have a very large number of distinguishable ethnic groups. For example, the Bureau of the Census has compiled a list of some 1,500 ethnic appellations in current use. But many ethnic groups are only sparsely represented in the United States, and among many others the sense of difference from ethnically adjoining groups is slight.

Clearly, ethnic identity has its roots in some historical community of people who inhabited a specific territory, developed a common language and culture, and practiced endogamy. The surprising feature of ethnic identity is its persistence for generations among those who left their homelands to mingle with other populations, as has been the case of immigrants to America.

According to an idea articulated as early as 1782 and gaining currency throughout the nineteenth and early twentieth centuries, America was destined to be a melting pot of immigrant ethnic groups, each losing its separate identity in a new blend that drew the best genetic and cultural qualities from its components.[3] The idea was so appealing to both the popular and scientific mind that contrary evidence was rarely noted. Throughout our history, conspicuous divisions have persisted between blacks, whites, Orientals, and Latins; between Protestants, Catholics, and Jews; and between Irish, Italians, English, and other national-origin groups. The divisions are reflected in ethnic endogamy, voluntary associations, and exclusionary practices in employment, education, and housing.

The requiem for the melting pot theory was finally pronounced by Glazer and Moynihan in 1963. *Beyond the Melting Pot,* their study of New York City's major ethnic groups, concluded that "the notion that the intense and unprecedented mixture of ethnic and religious groups in American life was soon to blend into a homogeneous end product has outlived its usefulness, and also its credibility. In the meantime, the persisting facts of ethnicity demand attention, understanding, and accommodation."[4] More recently, the same authors perceive a world-wide recrudescence of ethnicity as a principle of social and political organization.[5]

In America, the turn-of-the-century ideology of the melting pot has indeed lost ground to an alternative, the ideology of "cultural pluralism." Its adherents propose that rather than seeking to assimilate ethnic groups into a common American culture, we should work to preserve distinctive ethnic heritages because each tradition nourishes its members' self-esteem and adds flavor to our national life. During the past two decades, the rhetoric of ethnic activists has increasingly stressed the validity of their own traditions rather than the "Americanization" of their constituencies, and our schoolbooks have been rewritten accordingly.

However, the joke seems to be on the cultural pluralists. According to one thoughtful student of assimilation, most ethnic minorities have readily assimilated American culture even while maintaining their group identities. Milton Gordon cites an impressive body of sociological evidence supporting the proposition that the major cultural divisions in American today are along the lines of social class; regional and rural-urban distinctions, though once important, have greatly attenuated under the onslaught of modern mass communication and geographical mobility. Social classes also exist within ethnic groups; and the norms, aspirations, customs, and behavior of middle-class blacks, Jews, Puerto Ricans, white Catholics, and white Protestants are all both very much alike and considerably different from the common culture of their lower-class coethnics.[6]

In Gordon's view, cultural assimilation has generally preceded and need not be followed by "structural assimilation" as indicated by ethnically mixed participation in organizations and social relationships. On the contrary, "within the ethnic group there develops a network of organizations and informal social relationships which permits and encourages the members of the ethnic group to remain within the confines of the group for all of their primary relationships and some of their secondary relationships throughout all stages of the life-cycle."[7]

The result is a set of ethnically enclosed subsocieties, each more or less parallel in class structure and class culture (although the distribution of members among the classes varies considerably between ethnic groups, reflecting primarily the group's economic history).

Is Ethnicity Measurable?

Not all sociologists agree fully with Gordon's model of our national social structure as an orthogonal matrix of ethnicity and social class,[8] and Gordon himself offers qualifications that I have not detailed. But I find the model persuasive in accounting for many features of the American scene in 1980 and seminal in that it suggests what we should do to improve our understanding of the functional significance of ethnic identity in our society and its appropriate place in national policy. We need first to establish a reliable method of ethnic identification; then, for the numerically important ethnic groups, we should measure the degree of their ethnic enclosure.

A major impediment to the scientific classification of ethnic groups is the lack of a clearly specified membership rule. An individual's ethnic status is partly ascribed by his community from observation of his parentage, physical characteristics, language or mode of speech, organizational affiliations, and social circle. Some but not all these personal characteristics can be manipulated by the individual to reinforce or weaken the communal perception, so ethnicity is also partly an achieved status. An individual may place either a positive or negative value on his ascribed ethnicity, and in either case may consider his ethnic identity to be important or unimportant. A particular ethnic identity may not be consistently ascribed by others even when they have access to the same information about the subject individual, and self-identification may differ from the communally ascribed status.

When self-identification and communal identification agree, they are mutually reinforcing; when they disagree, the discord of mutual expectations generates a tension that is resolved only when one view or the other prevails. The problems of ethnic identification therefore focus on the marginal cases, whether of an individual who seeks to separate himself from a well-defined ethnic group or of a group that is itself disintegrating or merging with some adjoining ethnic group. For example, a reinterview study by the Bureau of the Census showed that people who identify themselves as Hispanic (versus non-Hispanic) in one interview often report differently in a second interview, and the reverse.[9] The same study shows that response consistency is strongly

related to ascertainable facts of family history such as the ethnic consistency of parental lineage and generational residence histories.

A general empirical study of ethnic self-identification and its objective correlatives would help considerably to resolve classification
problems and to guide the design of an ethnic questionnaire suitable
for mass administration, as in the decennial census. However, the systematic classification of ethnic groups also requires other information
concerning the functional importance of the nominated groups. Here I
think that a joint or parallel study of the degree of ethnic enclosure
would be critical. Let us say, for example, that we locate a group of
individuals who consistently identify themselves as Armenians. To
what degree do they form a separate subsociety whose members "remain within the confines of the group for all of their primary relationships and some of their secondary relationships throughout all stages
of the life-cycle"? Without going into detail, I suggest that the measurement of ethnic enclosure is fully within the state of the art of survey research. Given the appropriate data on a substantial sample of
the relevant populations, it would be feasible to develop a coherent
system of ethnic classification that reflected not only ethnic differences
but intergroup relationships. In short, such a study would reveal the
implicit ethnic structure of American society.

The final section of this essay suggests how such research might be
conducted. I should at this point reassure the reader that I do not suppose that the decennial census is an appropriate vehicle for gathering
all the information needed for such an ethnic analysis. Rather, I suppose that such an analysis would teach us how to better conduct an
ethnic census, just as quite detailed studies of social class have taught
us how to conduct more efficient surveys and censuses of socioeco-
nomic status.

Ethnic Identification in the Decennial Census

I began this essay by asserting that the Bureau's planning for the 1980
ethnic census lacked a solid foundation in science and that the absence
of science facilitated the intrusion of politics. Having dealt above with
the scientific issues, I turn now to the political ones. Beginning with a
few paragraphs of census history, I will try to illuminate the political
context of the 1980 ethnic enumeration.

The first decennial census was taken in 1790, pursuant to Article I,
Sec. 2 of the Constitution, which required a decennial enumeration of
the new nation's people as the basis for apportionment among the
states of both congressional representation and direct federal taxes.
That simple decennial enumeration grew into today's immense com-

pendium of demographic, social, and economic statistics. The expansion of the census's scope reflects a growing federal role in domestic affairs, a shifting agenda of national concerns, and the gradual legitimation of the social sciences.[10]

The first ethnic data (1790-1820) were essentially by-products of the distinction between white citizens (counted for representation and taxation) and others with fewer civil rights and liberties: foreigners not naturalized, slaves (presumably black), and tribal Indians, and on some early schedules, "all other free persons, except Indians not taxed." In 1830, the first nationally uniform schedule distinguished white from "colored" persons. In 1850, the concept of color was codified as white, black, or mulatto, and country of birth was first recorded for free inhabitants.

The censuses of 1870 and 1880 made a quantum leap in ethnic identification. In 1870, all inhabitants were classified as to color (white, black, mulatto, Chinese, or Indian) and country of birth, and it was recorded whether or not each parent was of foreign birth. In 1880, the specific country of birth was recorded for each parent, and a special census of the Indian population was conducted under the supervision of that giant of government science, John Wesley Powell. The Indian census schedule was interesting because it probed in an unprecedented way for ethnic identity, not just civil status.[11]

From 1890 through 1930 the census schedules gradually increased their attention to the complexities of ethnic identification, a response to the social and political issues raised by the swelling tide of immigration.[12] Each census recorded country of birth for the enumerated person and for both parents; and by 1920, language questions included "mother tongue" for all three persons. For the foreign-born, both the date of immigration and current civil status were reported. In 1930, the list of categories for "race and color" grew to include white, Negro, Mexican, Indian, Chinese, Japanese, Filipino, Hindu, and Korean, plus (for the first time) space for other write-in choices.

The census of 1960 was the first to use self-enumeration extensively.[13] The census schedule was consequently simplified and vetted for possibly offensive language, with some loss of precision. The former "color or race" question was replaced by one which read: "Is this person—White, Negro, American Indian, Japanese, Chinese, Filipino, Hawaiian, Part Hawaiian, Aleut, Eskimo, (etc.)?" The respondent had to induce the categorical structure within which identity was sought and write in an answer (rather than checking a box). Country of birth was included for the enumerated person and both parents; and for the enumerated person only, the mother tongue. In New York state only, a redundant nativity question distinguished "U.S., Puerto Rico,

Elsewhere" as places of birth, and asked whether those born "Else-where" were U.S. citizens.

Problems with the 1960 answers to the implicit color or race ques-tion prompted a return in 1970 to an explicit "color or race" query with checkoff entries for "white, Negro or black, Indian (Amer.), Japanese, Chinese, Filipino, Hawaiian, Korean, Other," with write-in space for a specified "other" or an Indian tribal designation. At some distance from the color or race question, the respondent was asked the state or country of birth for the enumerated person and his parents *and* to describe that person's "origin or descent" as one of the following:[14]

- Mexican
- Puerto Rican
- Cuban

- Central or South American
- Other Spanish
- No, none of these

For those who were foreign-born, the schedule asked whether they were now naturalized, aliens, or were born abroad of American citi-zens; when they "came to the United States to stay"; and "What lan-guage, other than English, was spoken in this person's home when he was a child?"

Playing the Numbers Game

Civil rights legislation and judicial decisions after 1960 bestowed a new significance on the Census Bureau's ethnic enumerations. A combina-tion of laws and executive orders prohibited discrimination based on race, color, religion, sex, or national origin in voter registration, educa-tion, public and private employment, privately owned public accom-modations, public facilities, the sale or rental of publicly assisted and most private housing, mortgage lending and property insurance, and in the selection of beneficiaries for federal grants under some 400 pro-grams administered by over 25 federal agencies.[15]

Whereas earlier statutes and judicial decisions had addressed problems of overt discrimination against specific individuals, the Con-gress and the courts went further in the 1960s, instructing federal au-thorities to look for patterns of discrimination as evidenced by the un-derrepresentation of "disadvantaged minorities" in the activity of interest and, where such underrepresentation was found, requiring "affirmative action" by the relevant party to correct it—whether or not the underrepresentation resulted from deliberate discriminatory policies.

The "pattern of discrimination" and "affirmative action" concepts together form a watershed in civil rights policy. Their underlying prin-ciple is that each minority group is entitled to a fair share of all "openings," whether ballots, jobs in a factory, seats in a classroom, apartments in a housing development, or food stamps. And each group's fair share is, basically, its share of the population at large or some relevant subset of that population.[16] By 1965, counting ethnic minorities had become a serious business, affecting the outcomes of elections, admission to graduate schools, marketing strategies of housing developers, federal contract awards, hiring, firing, and promotion policies of private employers, and the disbursement of federal grants to state and local governments.

I have yet to learn who decided, and on what basis, which ethnic minorities were candidates for affirmative action on their behalf. By whatever process, federal authorities settled on four such groups: American Indians or Alaskan Natives, Asian or Pacific Islanders, Blacks, and Hispanics. Whereas substantial underrepresentation of any of these groups is grounds for a civil rights compliance action, fair shares are not defined for any of the commonly distinguished components of each group (e.g., for Puerto Ricans as distinct from Mexican Hispanics) or for any ethnic minority not included in the "Big Four."[17]

Ethnic activists were quick to understand the practical significance of the fair-share principle: the larger the official count of their group's numbers, the greater would be the group's legal advantage in the competition for jobs, promotions, placement in training programs, housing, education, and access to federal benefits. So began the great numbers game of the 1970s.[18]

The census of 1970 was disappointing to ethnic activists in several respects. First, postcensal analysis convinced the Bureau that despite an excellent enumeration overall, the census substantially undercounted blacks (by 7.7 percent, versus 1.9 for whites) and probably Hispanics and Asian and Pacific Islanders.[19] The basic reasons were that within each minority group there was an above-average incidence of persons with irregular living arrangements (making them hard to locate), persons who could not read the Bureau's mailed messages (so did not learn about the purposes or even the existence of the census), persons who received census forms but did not complete and return them (because the form's intricacies were beyond their comprehension), and persons who had real or fancied reasons for being officially invisible (such as illegal aliens).

Second, the responses to the battery of ethnic questions did not allow the Bureau to say with confidence who belonged in which group. On about a tenth of the person-records, the question on "color or race" was unanswered. Write-in responses included many unclassifiable answers such as "American," racially uninformative national origins, hyphenated designations presumably reflecting mixed parentage, and other puzzlers.[20] It was often difficult to reconcile answers to the "color or race" question with answers to the "origin or descent," "place of birth," or "home-spoken language" questions. In postcensal reinterviews, respondents often answered differently than they did in the original enumeration.[21]

Ethnic spokesmen further speculated that their constituents often failed to recognize the category intended for them by the Bureau because they had developed different self-appellations (e.g., Chicano as opposed to Mexican or Spanish), and that some chose to misrepresent their ethnicity for ideological reasons ("Wherever my family came from, I'm an American now") or practical concerns (e.g., blacks who have "passed" as whites).

Finally, some ethnic activists were disappointed that the census schedule, the Bureau's coding guide, and tabulation formats jointly militated against identification of various ethnic groups that were arguably distinctive in their racial inheritance, social and economic status, culture, and aspirations.[22] Some reported themselves insulted as well as incensed by the Bureau's failure to draw finer distinctions.

When the Bureau began to plan the 1980 census, it formed advisory committees for the black, Spanish-origin, and Asian and Pacific-American populations. These groups addressed their inquiries and advice mainly to four salient issues: the Bureau's affirmative action employment plan; publicity and field procedures that would affect the completeness of minority enumeration; the format of ethnic questions on the 1980 census schedule; and the Bureau's plans for tabulating ethnic data. Each committee lobbied vigorously for measures that it believed would increase the 1980 count of its constituents or would make those constituents more visible in census reports.[23]

I think it is fair to say that the Bureau responded constructively to the often conflicting advice and occasional peremptory demands of its advisory committees. In a series of pretests, it experimented with publicity and expensive field procedures aimed at locating minority populations and persuading them to participate in the census. It also experimented with the format of questions related to ethnic identification, constrained as always by the space available on the census schedules and the cost and technical problems of coding open-ended responses. It was also constrained by a directive of the Office of Management and Budget (OMB) issued in May 1978.[24] OMB promulgated five basic racial and ethnic categories for federal statistics and program administrative reporting, whose definitions were as follows:

- *American Indian or Alaskan Native.* A person having origins in any of the original peoples of North America, and who maintains cultural identification through tribal affiliation or community recognition.
- *Asian or Pacific Islander.* A person having origins in any of the original peoples of the Far East, Southeast Asia, the Indian subcontinent, or the Pacific Islands. This area includes, for example, China, India, Japan, Korea, the Philippine Islands, and Samoa.
- *Black.* A person having origins in any of the black racial groups of Africa.
- *Hispanic.* A person of Mexican, Puerto Rican, Cuban, Central or South American or other Spanish culture or origin, regardless of race.
- *White.* A person having origins in any of the original peoples of Europe, North Africa, or the Middle East.

Although the directive encourages the separate reporting of "race" (designating all of the above except Hispanic as races) and "ethnicity" (Hispanic origin/not of Hispanic origin), Hispanic ethnicity takes precedence over race in a combined format. More detailed data may be collected but must be collapsible into the basic racial and ethnic categories listed above. Finally, OMB advises, "The category which most closely reflects the individual's recognition in his community should be used for purposes of reporting on persons who are of mixed racial and/ or ethnic origins."

Ethnic Identification in the 1980 Census

The census of 1980 continues the practice introduced in 1950 of using a short form for 100 percent enumeration and a longer form for a sample of respondents. The short form includes a "color or race" query (Q. 4) and an "origin or descent" query (Q. 7). The long form asks for country of birth (Q. 11), citizenship and date of immigration if foreign-born (Q. 12), domestic language and proficiency in spoken English (Q. 13), and ancestry (Q. 14). The long form, whose sample is adequate for national, state, and large SMSA estimates of fairly small populations, thus contains seven clues to ethnic identity.[25] Because the instrument is self-administered, the answers reflect a respondent's essentially unaided comprehension of the questions and his unguided perception of the appropriate responses. Generally, some adult member of the household is expected to complete the form on behalf of all its members, but friends, neighbors, volunteers, or census field staff may help those who seek help.

Ethnic lobbying for a place in the sun is most visible in Q. 4, which reads:

4. Is this person—   ○ White   ○ Asian Indian
   Fill one circle.   ○ Black or Negro   ○ Hawaiian
                           ○ Japanese   ○ Guamanian
                           ○ Chinese   ○ Samoan
                           ○ Filipino   ○ Eskimo
                           ○ Korean   ○ Aleut
                           ○ Vietnamese   ○ Other—*Specify*
                           ○ Indian (Amer.)   *Print tribe*

The fourteen listed options defy classification. Some items map rough- ly into traditional racial distinctions but at wildly different levels of classification. Others are more readily understood as national or terri- torial origins. Although only one choice is allowed, the entries are not necessarily mutually exclusive. For example, a respondent whose fa- ther was black and whose mother was white could choose either or both racial designations; or an Oriental living in Hawaii might con- sider himself both Chinese and Hawaiian. Anyone dissatisfied by the alternatives offered can write in some other appellation, but must in- tuit the relevant aspect of his/her identity.[26]

The intent of the short form's Q. 7 is somewhat clearer in that the options form a logically complete set:

7. Is this person of Spanish/   ○ No (not Spanish/Hispanic)
   Hispanic origin or   ○ Yes, Mexican, Mexican-Amer.,
   descent?   Chicano
   Fill one circle.   ○ Yes, Puerto Rican
                                 ○ Yes, Cuban
                                 ○ Yes, other Spanish/Hispanic

However, neither "Spanish/Hispanic" nor "origin or descent" are rig- orously defined in the accompanying instructions.[27] A respondent whose lineage, whatever its dominant ingredients, includes any indi- vidual born in one of the named countries (or any unnamed other "Spanish/Hispanic" country) is encouraged to identify himself as Hispanic.[28]

Long-form questions 11 through 13 ask for generally known or as- certainable facts: state or country of birth; citizenship status for the foreign-born; whether the enumerated person speaks a language other than English at home; and how well he speaks English. But Q. 14 seems to be a generalization of both Q. 4 and Q. 7, again lacking any clear categorical structure:

14. What is this person's ancestry? *If uncertain about how to report ancestry, see instruction guide.*

(For example: Afro-Amer., English, French, German, Honduran, Irish, Italian, Jamaican, Korean, Lebanese, Mexican, Nigerian, Polish, Ukranian, Venezuelan, etc.)

The instructions for answering this question, like those for Q. 7, legitimate a variety of choices for any respondent.[29] The Bureau has compiled a coding guide that allocates over 1,500 possible responses among nine geographical regions of the world, but with an overriding nongeographical "Spanish" category; and at a second level, among over 170 categories that are a mixture of smaller geographical areas, national states, and multinational ethnic groups.

Using 1980 Ethnic Statistics

My review of census schedules over the past three decades is intended to reveal what I perceive as the gradual articulation of the Bureau's stance on ethnic identification. Going beyond any language actually published by the Bureau,[30] I perceive its position to be as follows:

> Ethnic identity cannot be established by objective criteria, at least in large-scale self-administered surveys. We therefore accept that an individual's ethnicity is whatever he says it is. The Bureau's job is to elicit self-identification and then to group the responses into recognizable categories that (a) are mandated for federal civil rights enforcement, (b) satisfy the more vocal ethnic lobbies, and (c) provide enough continuity with past census statistics to satisfy social scientists engaged in longitudinal analysis.

In my judgment, the 1980 schedule's Q. 7, including its "tilt" in favor of Hispanic self-identification, responds quite directly to item (a) above.[31] The peculiar list of "racial" options in Q. 4 clearly reflects skillful lobbying by Asian and Pacific Islanders. Questions 10 through 14 of the long form are meant mainly to meet the needs of researchers, a constituency with which the Bureau has a long and mutually supportive relationship.

However, the Bureau's success in balancing the claims of constituencies was achieved at the expense of its fundamental mission—gathering valid and reliable information about the population of the United States. I see little reason to suppose that the 1980 census statistics will describe the ethnic composition of that population in a way that supports either fairness in civil rights enforcement or progress in the social sciences. One reason is that neither the Bureau nor its constituents has a coherent concept of ethnic identity to guide data collection and interpretation. A second reason is that the Bureau's own studies show a low order of response consistency in ethnic self-identification.

These concerns were shared by a census advisory panel appointed by the National Research Council, which reported in part as follows:[32]

> The nature of the (ethnic ancestry and Spanish origin) questions raises serious doubts about validity and reliability. Validity and reliability are dependent on the precision of the concept being measured. The phrases "origin or descent" and "ancestry" can refer to having one or more forebears from a particular country, or to nationality of a multinational country (*sic*), or to an ethnic identity (the referent most encountered in discussions of these questions). The discussions in the Panel make it clear that there were different interpretations of, or one could say confusion about, exactly what was being measured (validity). In the concrete, the answer will be what the respondent decides he or she is, or wants to be identified as, etc.
>
> It is by no means clear that persons in similar situations and with similar characteristics will answer in the same way. . . . We are speaking here not of splitting hairs, but of possibly wide variations in respondent behavior across and within generations and cultural groups leading to serious doubts about what the (ancestry) question measures or what its objective referent is. . . . The Spanish origin or descent question has some of the same problems.
>
> Reliability is important in two respects in regard to these questions. First, even if we accept the contention that the "truth" here is self-identification, would those in the household, especially adults and adolescents who do not fill out the census form, agree with the respondent? . . . Second, would the respondent identify himself or herself in the same way at a later time, if the census were taken at a different time of the year (e.g., St. Patrick's Day or Columbus Day) or if the respondent were not exposed to organized efforts to educate people to answer ethnic origin or ancestry questions in particular ways?

From the perspective of civil rights enforcement, there is something fundamentally wrong with the notion that ethnic status is elective. If one can gain advantages by claiming membership in a particular ethnic group, surely some of us will make unwarranted claims. Although ethnic self-identification in the census does not lead directly to advantages for each individual who reports himself as a member of a disadvantaged minority, the census's ethnic tabulations form the benchmark for many legal tests of ethnic underrepresentation. The larger the minority's count, the greater advantage all its members have in affirmative action programs.[33]

It is only fair to add that the Bureau of the Census does not make civil rights enforcement policy and cannot by itself resolve the intrinsic ambiguities of affirmative action. But neither is the Bureau required by law to choose ethnic self-identification as its criterion of classification. Both civil rights and science would be better served by a more analytical approach to data collection and dissemination.

From the perspective of social science, ethnic self-identification is indeed salient evidence of an individual's social identity. But for it to be scientifically useful evidence, three conditions must be met. First, self-identification must be elicited in an ethnically neutral context; the respondent must not be "led" to a choice among alternatives, none of which may in fact apply. Second, the intensity of an ethnic self-identification must be established by additional probes; for many who readily acknowledge a particular ethnic background, it is a trivial rather than salient element of self-concept. Third, self-identification must be analytically relatable to ascertainable facts about a person's life history, ancestry, and behavior; only as such relationships are established by statistical analysis do ethnic data acquire functional significance.

Improving the Census's Ethnic Statistics

The 1980 census schedule is now fixed, and the specific ethnic items on which the U.S. population reports as of April 1981 will be widely used both for public policy and academic research. Granted the doubts I share with the panel organized by the National Research Council and with some members of the Bureau's Advisory Committee on Population Statistics, what can be done to limit misinterpretation of the ethnic statistics that the Bureau will publish in due course? How should future censuses and intercensal surveys approach ethnic identification?

First, it is clearly appropriate to include in each publication that carries ethnic statistics a clear statement of the process that generated them and the reasons why they must be assumed to be imprecise. That statement should indicate that what was tabulated was the ethnic identities assigned to each member of a household by whomever completed the enumeration schedule; that the schedule guided respondents toward Hispanic identifications; and that response consistency, when it has been tested, is not much over 60 percent for some minorities.

Second, I urge a postcensal survey of ethnic identification that would serve two purposes: (a) it would clarify the meaning of the 1980 ethnic statistics; and (b) it would aid in designing future surveys and censuses.

An appropriate instrument for a postcensal probe of ethnicity would differ substantially from any that I have ever observed the Bureau using. First, its design would reflect a coherent analytical purpose, that of establishing a scale of intensity for ethnic self-identification and relating the scalar values insofar as possible to ascertainable facts about the respondents. Second, its format would reflect survey techniques that have been extensively used and evaluated in social-psychological surveys. These techniques include devices such as screening questions to eliminate respondents who do not have opinions about the matter at issue, nondirective probes for categories of self-identification, questions with scaled rather than dyadic responses, and redundant questions to test response consistency. There should be detailed questions about family lineage, languages, and residence history, and questions that measure the respondent's interaction with others of his ethnic group. The instrument should also ask about the respondent's religious heritage and affiliations, a topic that is statutorily excluded from the decennial census but is legally permissible in surveys to which response is not compulsory.

Although the Bureau is undoubtedly aware of the accomplishments of surveys using such social-psychological techniques,[34] it does not often use them. I am not sure of all the reasons; one, certainly, is concern about the reactions of congressional "know-nothings" who from time to time complain about the Bureau's nosiness. Another, I feel confident, is institutional conservatism; the Bureau has a solid reputation as our national fact-gatherer which it hesitates to contaminate by venturing into the softer area of attitude research. Finally, I am sure that there are some at the Bureau who are genuinely concerned about adverse public reactions to such probing inquiries—even though survey researchers generally agree that such reactions are rare among respondents.[35] In particular, one major Jewish organization and at least one minor Protestant denomination have officially opposed even noncompulsory religious censuses, at least if conducted by an agency of government.

Some who agree that a probing survey of ethnic identity would be socially and scientifically valuable nonetheless argue that such a survey would be more appropriately conducted by a less official scientific institution, such as an academic survey research center. However, there is an overriding technical objection to disconnecting such a survey from the Census Bureau. Because the survey's target is ethnic minorities, efficient sampling requires a sampling frame that identifies at least the nominal ethnicity of potential respondents. The decennial census provides not just the best but the only such national sampling frame. The impracticality of adequately sampling a number of small groups from the ethnically blind sampling frames available to academic researchers is one very good reason why research on ethnicity is meager.

My proposal, therefore, is that the Bureau use the returns from the decennial census to classify the nation's people according to nominal ethnic status, then sample as many of the minority groups as informed judgment and budgets allow. Next, each group should be surveyed, using a carefully designed, probing instrument to elicit both the intensity and objective correlatives of ethnic self-identification.[36]

I believe that the results of such a survey would substantially alter our current conceptions of the categorical structure and social significance of ethnic identity. From these findings, the Bureau could construct a less ambiguous and more efficient instrument for ethnic identification in future decennial censuses and sample surveys. The Bureau would be better equipped to resist pressure for favored treatment in instrument design from what we should expect to be an increasing number of ethnic lobbies with increasingly divergent interests. There is even some chance that the results of such a postcensal survey would be so startling that they would alter the political or legal premises of affirmative action. Most certainly, the findings would enhance our national understanding of the facts and social implications of "cultural pluralism" in American life.

NOTES

[1] This paper is a revision of one prepared originally for the annual meeting of the American Association for the Advancement of Science in San Francisco, California, 3-8 January 1980. It was presented at a session on "The 1980 Census: Plans, Procedures, Uses, and Evaluation," organized by Paul C. Glick. Mr. Glick and others at the Bureau of the Census were helpful in supplying documents and answering my questions. At Rand, Donna Betancourt helped me to locate sources and verify information; she also supervised production of this document. Arturo Gandara and Kevin F. McCarthy commented helpfully on the draft.

[2] In common speech, the term "ethnicity" has a variety of meanings, the most usual being "national origin." Thus the phrase "white ethnics" is often used to describe groups such as Italian- or Polish-Americans, a usage that appears in some scientific writing. Also ethnicity as a cultural distinction is sometimes contrasted with race as a genetic or morphological distinction. However, my usage is etymologically sound, has precedents in the literature of the social sciences, and is surpassingly convenient for this discussion.

[3] The history of the "melting pot" idea is well presented in Milton M. Gordon, *Assimilation in American Life* (New York: Oxford University Press, 1964), Ch. 5. I should acknowledge here that Gordon is my principal guide to the sociology of ethnic groups.

[4] Nathan Glazer and Daniel Patrick Moynihan, *Beyond the Melting Pot* (Cambridge: The M.I.T. Press and Harvard University Press, 1963), p. v.

[5] Nathan Glazer and Daniel P. Moynihan, eds., *Ethnicity: Theory and Experience* (Cambridge, Mass. and London: Harvard University Press, 1975), pp. 1-26.

[6] Gordon, *Assimilation in American Life,* pp. 40-59; illustrative material is presented in pp. 160-232.

[7] Ibid., p. 34.

[8] See William L. Yancey, Eugene P. Ericksen, and Richard N. Julian, "Emergent Ethnicity: A Review and Reformulation," *American Sociological Review* 41, No. 3 (June 1976): 391-403, both for the paper's argument and its helpful bibliography.

[9] U.S. Bureau of the Census, Census of Population and Housing: 1970, Evaluation and Research Program, PHC (E) -9, *Accuracy of Data for Selected Population Characteristics as Measured by Reinterviews,* (Washington, D.C.: U.S. Government Printing Office, 1974).

[10] Details of census schedules in the following paragraphs are taken from U.S. Bureau of the Census, *Population and Housing Inquiries in U.S. Decennial Censuses, 1790-1970,* Working Paper No. 39 (Washington, D.C., 1973).

[11] Enumerated persons are distinguished as to ancestral mixture (both tribal and non-Indian), languages spoken (both tribal and non-Indian), habitual clothing ("citizen's" vs. tribal dress), and residence on or off reservations; and non-Indian adoptees into Indian tribes are identified. See ibid., p. 69.

[12] During the peak decade, 1905-1914, over 10 million immigrants officially entered the United States, increasing the national population by an eighth. The census of 1920 enumerated nearly 14 million foreign-born residents in a population of 106 million.

[13] "Self-enumeration" must be interpreted loosely. A form is mailed or delivered to each household, covering all members of the household. Typically, the form is filled out by one member (sometimes even a non-member) on behalf of all members of the household.

[14] Independent of this question concerning Hispanic origin or descent, the Bureau also coded respondents with Hispanic surnames.

[15] The principal laws were the Civil Rights Act of 1964 (PL 88-352), the Voting Rights Act of 1965 (PL 89-110), the Civil Rights Act of 1968 (PL 90-284), the Equal Employment Opportunity Act of 1972 (PL 92-261), and the Voting Rights Act of 1975 (PL 94-73). The principal executive orders were 11063 (Equal Opportunity in Housing), 1962; 11246 (Equal Employment Opportunity), 1965; 11478 (Equal Employment Opportunity in the Federal Government), 1969; and 11764 (Nondiscrimination in Federally Assisted Programs), 1974.

[16] The general principle has many qualifications that are specific to the various statutes and regulations. Most qualifications center on the appropriate definition in a particular case of the population which is "at risk" of discrimination. For example, ethnic underrepresentation in employment by a particular firm may be tested with reference to the ethnic composition of the labor force living in the firm's vicinity and already possessing the relevant skills; or the base may include all those plausibly trainable for the jobs in question. The firm's labor market may be determined to vary with job classification, from local to national.

[17] The Office of Federal Contract Compliance Programs does recognize possible discrimination in executive and middle-management jobs against "members of various religious and ethnic groups primarily but not exclusively of Eastern, Middle, and Southern European ancestry, such as Jews, Catholics, Italians, Greeks, and Slavic groups," but its compliance guidelines for employ-

ers do not (yet?) include the arithmetical tests provided for the Big Four (41 *Code of Federal Regulations* 60-50).

[18] The nature of the game is neatly captured in a recent interchange between the Bureau, the National Black Caucus of Elected Officials, and a prominent Mexican-American politician. At a meeting of the caucus, Larry Lucas, a Bureau spokesman, predicted that Hispanics would not outnumber blacks in the U.S. until the year 2057. According to a press report, "Eddie Williams (a member of the caucus) said talk of a fast-growing Hispanic population, with its potential Hispanic political gains, has 'created some tensions between blacks and Hispanics.' Although black and Hispanic leaders are unhappy about it, the politics of poverty have put the two groups in competition for their share of dwindling federal dollars. And, as Lucas told the local officials, the census is 'involved in how the national pie is cut up'." (*Los Angeles Times,* 26 November 1979.)

Within a few days, the Bureau's projection was hotly disputed by Mario Obledo, California's Secretary of Health and Welfare, who took the Bureau to task for underenumerating Hispanics and predicted that "Hispanics will be the largest minority group in this country sometime before the end of the century." (*Los Angeles Times,* 30 November 1979).

[19] U.S. Bureau of the Census, Census of Population and Housing: 1970, Evaluation and Research Program, PHC (E) -4, *Estimates of Coverage of Population by Sex, Race, and Age: Demographic Analysis* (Washington, D.C.: U.S. Government Printing Office).

[20] Tabulations of the long form administered to a 5 percent sample of households originally indicated that the sample equivalent of 517,000 persons had reported some racial designation other than those explicitly named on the census schedule. Editors subsequently reclassified three-fifths of these cases as "white." (Ibid., p. 4.)

[21] For example, about 18 percent of those who reported Spanish origin or descent in the original enumeration reported otherwise upon reinterview; and 23 percent who were so identified at reinterview were reported as non-Spanish in the original interview. Both calculations exclude nonrespondents. (U.S. Bureau of the Census, Census of Population and Housing: 1970, Evaluation and Research Program, PHC (E) -9, *Accuracy of Data for Selected Population Characteristics as Measured by Reinterviews* (Washington, D.C.: U.S. Government Printing Office, 1974), Table D.

[22] For example, in 1978 a representative of the Taiwanese Club of America pointed out to the Bureau, "The number of Taiwanese-Americans in this country is approaching 100,000. . . . These immigrants have their own unique social background. Their educational level, spoken language, and cultural tradition are grossly different from those of the early Chinese immigrants. . . . The majority of Taiwanese do not want to be called 'Chinese.'" (U.S. Bureau of the Census, *Minutes and Report of Committee Recommendations, Census Advisory Committee on the Asian and Pacific-American Population for the 1980 Census,* 9 November 1978, p. 31.)

[23] The *Minutes and Report of Committee Recommendations* of the three committees were published by the U.S. Bureau of the Census at intervals during 1977-79. The Bureau apparently offered to charter an American Indian Advisory Committee, but the leaders of that constituency preferred less formal consultation.

[24] The National Archives of the United States, *Federal Register,* Vol. 43, No. 87, pp. 19269-70. 25. It does not include the 1970 items on country of birth for the parents of the enumerated person. The census last asked about the parents' "mother tongues" in 1920.

[25] It does not include the 1970 items or country of birth for the parents of the enumerated person. The census last asked about the parents' "mother-tongues" in 1920.

[26] The instruction sheet to accompany the mailed-out census schedule is not very helpful. Apropos of Q. 4, it says: "Fill the circle for the category with which the person most closely identifies. If you fill the 'Indian (Amer.)' or 'Other' circle, be sure to print the name of the specific Indian tribe or specific group."

[27] The instructions for Q. 7 read as follows: "A person is of Spanish/Hispanic origin or descent if the person identifies his or her ancestry with one of the listed groups, that is, Mexican, Puerto Rican, etc. Origin or descent (ancestry) may be viewed as the nationality group, the lineage, or country in which the person or the person's parents or ancestors were born."

[28] As the Bureau's review of the 1970 "origin or descent" responses notes, "If a person had Spanish ancestry on one side of the family several generations back, he may or may not perceive himself to be of Spanish origin when reporting on the census questionnaire. . . . Since the question may have been answered on the basis of the respondent's self-perception, the idea of a 'correct' or 'incorrect' response does not seem to apply." (U.S. Bureau of the Census, *Accuracy of Data for Selected Population Characteristics as Measured by Reinterviews,* p. 5.) I am told that the Bureau also plans, as in 1970, to flag Spanish surnames (it has a list of some 8,500 such surnames) and tabulate their incidence as an alternative measure of the Hispanic population. In the past, Spanish surname has not correlated very well with self-identified Hispanic origin or descent.

[29] "Print the ancestry group with which the person identifies. Ancestry (or origin or descent) may be viewed as the nationality group, the lineage, or the country in which the person or the person's parents or ancestors were born before their arrival in the United States. Persons who are of more than one origin and who cannot identify with a single group should print their multiple ancestry (for example, German-Irish)."

"Be specific; for example, if ancestry is 'Indian,' specify whether American Indian, Asian Indian, or West Indian. Distinguish Cape Verdean from Portuguese, and French Canadian from Canadian. A religious group should not be reported as a person's ancestry."

[30] But see comments by Jacob S. Siegel, senior statistician, and Daniel B. Levine, associate director for demographic fields, in U.S. Bureau of the Census, *Minutes and Report of Committee Recommendations,* Census Advisory Committee on Population Statistics, 6 April 1979, pp. 19-24.

[31] Compare the instructions for Q. 7 with the OMB directive on racial and ethnic reporting, supra.

[32] Panel on Decennial Census Plans, Committee on National Statistics, Assembly of Behavioral and Social Sciences, National Research Council, *Counting the People in 1980: An Appraisal of Census Plans* (Washington, D.C.: National Academy of Sciences, 1978), pp. 67-76; the quoted sentences are from pp. 71-72.

[33] In affirmative action programs, the numerators of ethnic participation rates are even more unreliable than the denominators. For instance, under the rules of the Equal Employment Opportunity Commission, employers engaged in affirmative action compliance are forbidden to ask job applicants their ethnic identities until after they have been hired; and are discouraged from doing so then. Typically, an ethnic identity is assigned to each employee by his employer, based on whatever clues can be found in physiognomy, speech pat-

terns, name, and place of birth. Employees rarely know how they have been classified.

[34] In fact, over a decade ago, the Bureau sponsored a conference on "*Survey Applications of Social Psychological Questions*" (reported by Norman W. Storer, and published under the above title as U.S. Bureau of the Census Working Paper 29, Washington, D.C., 1969). According to the introduction, "The immediate occasion for taking up this general topic is the increasing involvement of the Census Bureau, especially through its current population survey, in collecting data relevant to new social programs in such areas as poverty, manpower training, education, urban redevelopment, and health care." Despite the generally positive conclusion of the conferees, the Bureau did not subsequently make much use of "social-psychological questions" in its surveys, even those conducted under contract to other federal agencies.

[35] The conference report cited above notes, "Experience in the field has shown consistently that respondents are much less likely to be disturbed by questions that are sensitive (i.e., whose answers might embarrass or humiliate the respondent) than are their "public protectors"—Congressmen, spokesmen for ethnic groups, the American Civil Liberties Union (ACLU), etc. No good examples could be offered by the discussants of questions that have elicited widespread hostility from respondents, or even that have met with a high proportion of refusals to answer." (Ibid., p. 1.)

[36] Although both instrument design and sampling for such a survey are well within the state of the art, field procedures would present some formidable difficulties. The sampled households would be widely dispersed geographically, a substantial number would have moved from their April 1980 addresses, and language barriers would complicate interviewing.

The New Immigration: Its Origin, Visibility, and Implications for Public Policy[1]

Roy Simon Bryce-Laporte

Research Institute on Immigration and Ethnic Studies
Smithsonian Institution

Introduction

The United States of America is a country where history is conventionally defined as one of immigration and immigrants—a claim which, if true, holds for all of the Americas as well. The United States is a society which persists in operating largely on the bases of ethnic distinctions and cultural differences, despite myths to the contrary. Surely there are other modes of orientation, organization, and stratification in American society; however, for many interests and issues, people identify themselves or are identified, treat others and are treated, act and are affected on the basis of their perceived or actual ethnicity. Everyone is perceived, then, as having some ethnic category or as pertaining to some ethnic or racial group (the two not necessarily being the same, although they have come to be treated so in the United States).

Historically, immigration has been one of the principal contributing factors to the ethnic configuration of this nation. Insofar as immigration has never ceased to occur in the United States, ethnicity has never desisted in operating within the social order. There are, of course, other bases and causes for the perpetuation of ethnicity other than immigration. Periods of rise and fall occur in the articulation of ethnicity as a phenomenon or public issue which may not be connected to immigration *per se;* also there are other social consequences and manifestations of immigrants that may be considered independent of immigration. Even when all these exceptions are conceded, ethnicity, immigration and the relationship between them are irrefutably pertinent to any appreciation of the internal as well as external complexities of the contemporary United States. Thus this relationship continues to have some telling impacts or implications for the direction of policy-making on various levels of government. Conversely, various levels of public policy themselves affect the direction of immigration and ethnic-oriented actions.

The objectives of this essay are: (1) to review patterns of recent immigration into the United States; (2) assess its impacts as a phenomenon upon U.S. ethnic configurations and the distribution of socio-cultural characteristics associated with that immigration; (3) distinguish the impacts of the phenomenon of immigration from the issues and images of immigration; and (4) in so doing, discuss the recent implications of immigration phenomenon for various interconnecting levels of public policy considerations.

For purposes of this essay, immigration may be defined as the movement of aliens into the United States and its overseas jurisdictions who establish indefinite, long-term or permanent residence therein and proceed to operate in whole or in part within the rights granted to persons legally so designated. In that sense, immigration to the United States can be divided into three main categories: legal; parole; and illegal. The first represents persons who enter the country according to established law and have thereafter been granted legal status of permanent residents or resident aliens, with permission to exercise all rights, privileges, and obligations associated with that category. Second are those persons who enter the country legally, generally as political refugees or disaster victims as defined by a particular legislative act or statutory authority of the U.S. government, and are granted certain limited rights of stay, activities, and government support beyond that permitted to non-immigrants. Third are those persons who enter the country fraudulently, or who having entered legally as non-immigrants, proceed to violate that status by either overstaying the period of time granted them or pursuing under false pretenses activities normally limited to legal residents or U.S. citizens.

Falling somewhere outside the definition stipulated above are other categories of immigrants such as (1) naturalized American citizens who resided previously in a foreign country or formerly had a non-U.S. nationality, (2) persons of alien birth or nationality who came to the United States as non-immigrants and continue to hold this category and adhere to the restrictions associated with it, (3) resident aliens or American citizens who change their place of residence from one region to another within the country as part of internal geographical mobility or leave the country temporarily and return, (4) U.S. extraterritorial or colonial migrants, (5) U.S. expatriates, alien deportees, and other aliens who leave the United States permanently, (6) U.S. citizens living or doing military service abroad, and (7) aliens who have applied for entry as well as those who have received visas but not yet arrived in this country.

No complete picture of the ethnic configuration of American society as influenced by immigration could ever be arrived at without considering all the above mentioned categories and their interrelationships. Obviously, some categories affect the ethnic configurations more directly and clearly than others; some are more useful for research while others are more central to policy. For instance, internal and secondary migrations may affect ethnic distribution; entry, naturalization, natural growth, adoption, or death of legal immigrants also affect the country's ethnic composition. While legal immigrants may affect policy openly and directly, parolees may do so sensationally but obliquely; illegals may affect it surreptitiously; non-immigrants represent potentials for the growth in number of either legal or illegal immigrants.

We may ask what would be the ethnic, indeed the general, situation of this nation if all the above categories were held constant, equivalent and at a maximum rate or volume? If all emigres from the United States returned to this country, all visa applicants were admitted, and all illegals and refugees were given permanent status automatically, if there were no deportations and legal immigrants remained and became United States citizens automatically, if all aliens produced large families which remained in the U.S. permanently, and if the entire U.S. population would live forever while the present economic crises and world conditions remained unchanged, what would be the societal cost?

Hypothetically, any or all of these could occur. Obviously if all did, the country could face irreconcilable, disastrous crises. While such is, of course, not the actual or likely situation, it is precisely these kinds and combinations of absurdities and fears which are assumed, publicized, and often manipulated in the anti-immigration campaign in order to dramatize the presence of new immigrants (really new ethnics), to arouse the public, and to influence policymakers against them.

Too much politicking and too much policy dickering take place in response to provocative, contrived public issues. Too little politics and too little policy-making are based on the knowledge we have (or require) about the complexity of immigration as a phenomenon. To the extent, therefore, that immigration becomes the basis for deciding or influencing ethnic-related policies or the object of such policies, it compounds those tasks. This is true because immigration in itself is so complex and little known. Much concerning it is assumed rather than analyzed.

All of the above does not deny the value and importance of studying immigration as a public or policy issue at this time. Indeed, many aspects of the contemporary immigration phenomenon result from tacit as well as explicit policy decisions and legislation (or the failure to make and implement them). But much of today's policy considerations are reactions not to immigration as a phenomenon but as a public issue; and sometimes the public issue emerges as a reaction to myths and manipulations of the image of immigration. Thus it is important for analytical reasons to keep the phenomenon of immigration clear— even if not separate—from the public issues and images associated with it.

As a phenomenon, immigration is a complex, constantly changing part of a continuing historical and human process. It is one of the ongoing modes of peopling the United States, shaping its ethnic cultural configurations, and establishing linkages between it and the rest of the world. Although it is a universal form of human behavior, immigration is not mysterious, mechanistic or random; although an incessant phenomenon in the formation of the United States as a national society and in the structuring and evolving of its international political economy, immigration has not been a constantly salient public issue in the social and political history of this country. Sometimes its distinctions—as the phenomenon of an issue or the images of one—are not easily recognized, any more than are other distinctions such as those between motives and conditions of immigrants, forms and functions of immigration, reactions of government and public to immigration, or immigrants in different situations or stages of development.

The Phenomenon of the New Immigration

Based on most recent archaeological findings, it was at least twelve thousand years ago that human populations first immigrated and settled in what today is viewed as the continental United States. With the states of Hawaii and Alaska included, it is perhaps more than fifty thousand years since the first human immigrants entered this country. Controversies exist about the first European and African presence in this hemisphere. Certainly they occurred nowhere as early as the coming of the first Americans (the so-called American "Indians"), at least among those who accept the notion that the latter also immigrated here from distant lands. "Colonists," "slaves," "servants," "strangers" were terms of reference for those who came to the country from the period of its early European colonization through its independence. The term "immigrant" was a relative latecomer to North American parlance; it emerged as part of the postindependence or early nationalistic vocabulary by which foreigners were recognized and differentiated from nationals.

From 1820 through 1979 there has been registration of 48,664,965 alien persons who entered the United States as immigrants or who later changed their status from non-immigrant to immigrant (according to the U.S. Department of Justice, 1978). There has been no year in which official immigration into the country has not occurred; the lowest ever being 6,354 in 1823 and the highest 1,285,349 in 1907. There have been, however, periods of discrete clusters of entering immigrants which often were characterizable by the specificity of their conditions, crises, and contingencies. In contemporary times the last significantly low period was from 1931 to 1945, the period of the Great Depression and World War II. There has been a rather high entry rate ever since then, and a distinct increase can be observed since the mid-1960s. The count of entering legal immigrants in 1968 reached 400,000 for the first time since World War II. By fiscal year 1978 the count reached 601,442 persons, a figure which was last superceded in 1924.

This increase since the mid-1960s is referred to as the "new immigration." However, more accurately is "another new immigration," since every wave of immigrants is so termed by those who preceded them. Legally this one is earmarked by the congressional passage of the Immigration and Naturalization Act of 1965, although some anticipatory movements began in the years immediately before its enactment. The act itself is new in terms of shifts in its provisions relative to its predecessors; the immigration is new not only in terms of recency and volume, but because of the predominant source of countries involved and distinctive characteristics of the people who comprise it.

Until 1965, legal immigration into the United States was governed basically by an act passed by Congress in 1924 and later amended by the McCarran Act of 1952. The first quota act was passed in 1921 as a stopgap measure to curtail the rush of immigration at the end of World War I. Its successor, the Act of 1924, created a national origin quota system designed to allow for immigration, but along lines which would basically retain established ethnic proportions and favor the highest representations coming from countries which provided the United States with its earliest European settlers, those from Western and Northern Europe.

This now defunct system limited the quota of each nation to an equal ratio of 150,000 of the number of inhabitants of that same nationality already in the United States as determined by the 1920 census. Theoretically, this arrangement favored a high inflow by Western and Northern Europeans over their Southern and Eastern counterparts, due to the latter's light representation in the country's earlier settlement. Orientals were already restricted to entry as laborers due to legislation in 1917. Moreover, dependencies in many areas of the non-European world were each restricted to 200 entries per year. Only the independent countries of the Western Hemisphere were granted generally unlimited entry.

After a number of piecemeal legislations, a new act was passed in 1965. It was the most comprehensive alteration of immigration laws for the country since the basic 1924 law, and is still the basic legislation which governs present immigration policies and patterns. The Immigration and Naturalization Act of 1965 was Congress's reaction to domestic pressures for expanding further opportunities to enter the United States legally; it was also a response to the changing world situation and pressing desire of peoples from outside the Western and Northern European regions to become part of the historical stream of immigrants which comprised the United States.

More specifically, the 1965 act replaced the single-nation quota system with one based on hemispheric ceilings. It abolished restrictions against Asian and Pacific peoples, while imposing a limit on the Western Hemisphere. It instituted a first-come, first-served system of admission within a set of preferences, and it freed close relatives of U.S. citizens from numerical ceilings. The Eastern Hemisphere was assigned an annual ceiling of 170,000 immigrants, with a limit of 22,000 per independent country. The Western Hemisphere was assigned a ceiling of 120,000 per annum without quotas for independent nations. Later limits on the latter were expanded and family preferences adjusted in order to establish greater equity between hemispheric origins.

One objective behind the act was to alleviate the admittedly anti-Asian bias of previous legislation and policies. In the case of the Western Hemisphere, however, the objective may have been more than the matter of establishing equity with the Eastern Hemisphere. It seemed intended also to check the already noticeably growing inflow of peoples from largely non-white countries of Latin and non-Latin makeup located south of the U.S. border. Fear was voiced in some circles about the multiple and far-reaching implications of population movements from these countries into the United States. The fear suggests that there was serious apprehension in those circles toward the growing presence and potential pressures of people from countries with delicately close geographical, political, and economic relations with the United States. These peoples were also perceived as different, perhaps inferior racially, culturally and socially, and economically threatening or politically dangerous. Thus ethnic consideration and ethnocentrism entered early in the formulation of the present immigration act, even though the original legislation in itself was more egalitarian than any of its predecessors.[1] Yet, it is not only true that ethnicity affects or enters into the formulation of immigration policy, but that immigration also affects ethnic-oriented public policy.

Impact of the Immigration and Naturalization Act of 1965

Legal Immigration

With the emergence of the recent crises associated with the flotilla of Cuban and Haitian "boat peoples," much more attention is directed today to illegal immigrants, political refugees, and parolees than to the legal emigres who settle in this country. Much of the news is sensational, and comments are speculative about these kinds of immigrants and immigration into the United States. This heavy stress on illegal immigration, and now on refugees, has led to either oblivating or distorting the case of legal immigrants and therefore of U.S. immigration and its related ethnic reality.

Legal immigrants pose some distinctive reasons for further attention. Among other things, legal immigrants can participate, make demands, and contribute openly in U.S. society. Immigrants, those entering with permanent visas and, to a lesser degree, dependents and refugees, enjoy many rights in this country—permanent residence, employment, welfare, public services, and social security benefits. They pay taxes, are susceptible to military call, or can enter into voluntary service. The restrictions they experience pertain to their ineligibility for (1) certain employment opportunities in the federal and local governments, and (2) such political rights as jury service and voting for or holding public office. After a fixed period of residence and certain other considerations, legal immigrants become eligible for naturalization to American citizenship. The acquisition of citizenship then opens to them most political rights enjoyed by native-born citizens, except occupation of the presidency of the United States. Therefore, they are de jure components of the American population; they represent constituencies of public officials; they are legitimate clients of certain public services and prestigious private organizations. Thus legal immigrants should not be conceived of merely as active additions to the national population, but also as potential new citizens to the country.

Throughout U.S. history, alien residents as well as those who later became naturalized citizens have made important contributions to the society, not only to its demography but also to its culture, arts, sports, economics, technology, politics, and defense. The current historical period is also characterized by significant leadership roles played by individuals of foreign birth, such as Henry Kissinger and Zbigniew Brzezinski in diplomacy, Dr. James Haughton and Dr. Charles Gerald in public health, Chien Fhiung Wu in physics, Vidia Naipul in letters, Carlos Quintero, Sidney Poitier, and Harry Belafonte in theater arts, Sir Arthur Lewis, Kenneth B. Clark, and Elliot Skinner in academia, Zubin Mehta, Rogue Cordero, and Ozawa in classical music, Celia Cruz, Mongo Santamaria, Bob Marley, and Billy Cogham in popular music, Calypso Rose and Jonas dos Santos in folk arts, Geoffrey Holder and Alvin Ailey in dance, and Rodney Carew and Edson Arantes de Nascimento (Pele) in sports. Some individuals among the foreign-born have acquired leading political and governmental positions on local and regional levels, e.g., Trinidadian-born Mervyn Dymally as a congressman and a former Lieutenant Governor of California, and Panamanian-born Edward Griffith and Waldaba Stewart as state legislators in New York. Compared to their illegal peers, then, legal immigrants exercise very open, active, profound, and long-lasting impacts on American society. This is true not only of outstanding individuals but of them all as a sociological category.

According to INS data, legal immigrants (including status-changers) totaled 3,494,143 persons in the pre-1965 act period (1953-65) and 5,270,016 persons in the post-act period (1966-78), an increase of 50.82%. On the hemispheric level, the Eastern Hemisphere provided a total of 1,828,974 legal immigrants, comprising 52.34% of the world's total contributions to U.S. immigration in the pre-act period, and 2,913,746, or 55.29% of the world's contribution in the post-act period. The Western Hemisphere provided 1,465,754, or 47.66%, and 2,350,270, or 44.71%, in the pre- and post-act periods respectively. In both periods the Eastern Hemisphere was the leading source of immigrants, although the margin of difference decreased slightly in the post-act period.

On the continental level, Europe contributed 1,732,346, or 49.58% of the world total in the pre-act period, but only 1,282,779, or 24.34% in the post-act period. Asia provided 256,742, or 7.35% of the world total in the pre-act period, but 1,501,653, or 28.49% in the post-act period. Europe, then, lost its position as the leading source of legal immigrants to the U.S. in the post-act period to North America and Asia in descending order. It is the only continent which suffered a loss—of 449,567 persons, or 25.95%—while Asia experienced a stupendous increase of 1,244,911 persons, or 400.89%.

On the national level, the countries which provided the leading number of citizens as immigrants to the U.S. for the pre-act period of

1953-1960 were as follows in descending order: Mexico, 526,452
(15.17% of the world total); Canada, 400,793 (11.47%); Germany,
339,605 (9.72%); United Kingdom, 305,252 (8.74%); Italy, 255,168
(7.30%); Cuba 150,597 (4.31%); Poland 101,564 (2.91%); Ireland,
86,885 (2.49%); Hungary 60,748 (1.74%); and the Netherlands
59,396 (1.70%). In the post-act period the order is as follows: Mexico
732,575 (13.90%); Cuba 479,459 (9.10%); Philippines 352,528
(6.69%); Italy, 240,538 (4.56%); Korea 229.119 (4.35%); Canada
196,834 (3.73%); United Kingdom 195,298 (3.71%); China-Taiwan
187,291 (3.55%); Dominican Republic 169,434 (3.22%); and Jamaica
163,913 (3.00%). A closer examination shows that Germany, Poland,
Ireland, Hungary and the Netherlands suffered sufficient enough decreases in rank as contributors to U.S. immigration in the second period to be dropped from the list of leading immigration sources. They
were replaced in the category by the Philippines, Korea, China-Taiwan, Dominican Republic, and India. Canada and the United Kingdom suffered 50.89% and 36.02% losses in output respectively and
also in rank, but retained their membership among the ten leading
contributors of citizens to U.S. immigration. Italy suffered a slight reduction in volume (75.80%) but rose in rank; Cuba gained in volume
(218.37%) and rank; and Mexico gained in volume (39.15%) and
maintained its leadership of source countries.

   Of those countries which were named in both the pre- and post-act
periods, only Mexico and Cuba actually increased their percentage of
the world total contribution in the post-act period; the others suffered
proportional losses. The spread among the top ten leading source
countries was narrower, and the proportion of immigrants represented
by the leaders was less in the pre-act compared to the post-act period.
Other countries producing 100,000 or more nationals as U.S. legal immigrants in the post-act period, but which fell just outside of the top
ten category, were India with 157,624, Greece with 152,214, Germany
with 120,561, and Vietnam with 116,258.

Non-Immigrants, Parolees, and Undocumented Aliens

In addition to its legal component, the "new immigration" is comprised of non-immigrants, parolees, and so-called illegals or undocumented workers (although technically the two last terms are not always congruous). Aside from the functioning of all three of these
categories as resource pools from which legal immigrants are obtained
via legal procedures for status changes—and in the case of some parolees facilitating their early acquisition for citizenship—their members

participate in the everyday life, economics, culture and politics of the society. They are part of the populace, and no less a linkage than their legal counterparts between the United States and its present or future international neighbors. In some cases, members of these groups have succeeded in influencing the national and local political processes of the United States, and are becoming involved in critical actions by the federal government, especially its diplomatic, military, and intelligence sectors.

According to INS data, 9,343,710 non-immigrants (including 1,041,142 returning resident aliens) were admitted in 1978 into the country. The total number of non-immigrants admitted in 1978 was about fifteen times the number of legal immigrants for the same year. Only five of the leading source countries (Mexico, United Kingdom, Canada, Colombia, and Italy) register among the leading sources of non-immigrants for the year 1978. The same five are also among the leading source of legal immigrants for the post-act period.

Parolees have been a part of the larger tradition of granting asylum to mostly political refugees. The categories of parolees and refugees are not exactly congruent. In recent times, the parolee category has come to mean largely persons fleeing communist or other perceived repressive "anti-American" *political* systems who specifically receive special aid and privileges from the U.S. government during their stay and are facilitated in their efforts to gain residence and citizenship. A total of 1,324,670 persons have been admitted into the United States in this category between 1846 and 1978 based on various special legislative acts that authorized their admission. INS reports that the figure of 132,781 refugees admitted to the United States in 1979 does not include the estimated 100,000 Cubans and 20,000 Haitians who recently entered this country by way of Florida.

There are several other Latin American and Asian countries whose conditions merit acceptance of their refugees as parolees on human rights grounds, but international and domestic interests of the United States rule it quite unlikely that they will be so treated. In addition to illegals—as the Iranian crisis revealed—quite a number of refugees from countries with non-communist governments friendly to the United States may be hidden within nebulous categories such as students or trainees as a mode of creating a safety valve.

Illegals are by definition an elusive category subject to a very wide variation in estimates. Generally, such estimates are based or extrapolated from undocumented or improperly documented aliens arrested and detained while performing labor without legal permission or crossing the border illegally. Estimates have ranged from two to ten million. The largest estimates tend to come from groups with interests in mak-

ing claims of massive presence of illegals in the country. The estimates
are also skewed because they are based not on actual numbers and
types of aliens deported or asked to leave the United States, but on
illegal immigrants arrested and confined in special detention camps.
More likely, then, such data suggest that certain kinds or locations of
business draw upon illegal or undocumented immigrant labor which
are intermittently raided by police and immigration authorities. Such
data do not provide reliable evidence for determining number, distribution, or composition of the general illegal immigrant population of
this country and its territories, but only of those who are most likely to
be apprehended and detained in these camps.

The Domestic Council on Illegal Aliens reported the following countries as comprising the principal sources of illegal aliens to the United
States: Mexico; Dominican Republic; Haiti; Jamaica; Guatemala; Colombia; Peru; Ecuador; Philippines; Korea; Thailand; Greece; India;
Iran; and Nigeria. Note may be taken here again of the reappearance
of many countries which also figure as leading sources of legal immigration. In fact, of the above mentioned, only Guatemala, Thailand,
and Ecuador are not listed as leading sources of legal immigrants. The
Haitians and their sympathizers have been contesting the former being assigned "illegal" status, claiming these refugees are political and
not only "economic" refugees.

Under closer examination, some kind of interconnectedness is
strongly suggested among the major types of immigration—legal immigrants, non-immigrants, parolees and illegals. With the exception of
a country in a highly favorable economic stage of development such as
Japan, most source countries of legal immigrants are also high sources
of non-immigrants and illegal immigrants. The latter two are residual
categories of surplus immigrants who would have come and stayed legally if U.S. law and policy or their implementation would have so permitted, thus reflecting more closely the volume and intensity of those
desiring entrance into this country. Seen behaviorally then, their illegal status is a function of a legally created restraint which may be
counterproductive in terms of the family reunification objective of
present policies. The parolees tend to come from countries which may
have been the sources of high numbers of legal immigrants; if legal
restraints were imposed on them, they would have been highly represented among the illegal immigrants as well. The same is true for many
of the extraterritorial or colonial migrants who would also have to be
classified as legal or illegal immigrants had their countries been "independent" of the U.S.; they might have been included among the parolees if their countries were dominated by communist governments.

To summarize, the impact of the 1965 Act has been significant demographically in many ways. There has been an increase in the volume and rate of entry of immigrants, as well as an expansion and facilitation of entry for categories of immigrants not appropriately provided for in earlier acts. Moreover, there has been a marked increase in the entry of immigrants not legally provided for, and at rates or under conditions not appropriately addressed by the Act itself. Finally, doors have been opened to nationalities and ethnics previously disallowed by law, and there has been a rearranging of the composition and order of the leading source countries of immigration into the United States.

The Visibility Factor Among New Immigrants

In addition to the largely demographic considerations stated above, there are other characteristics and trends among the new immigrants which could have very serious impacts on U.S. society. One of these is the sharp visibility[3] of these new groups relative to the older groups of immigrants, and the impact it will have on the heterogeneity and ethos of the society. By visibility is meant here the degree of observable (often considered rejectionable) distinctiveness a given human group possesses or displays, relative to the majority group in the larger population.

There are various bases and kinds of visibility. The range falls from certain obvious, generalized phenotypical features which may be impossible to lose or obscure, to other traits on the level of traditional symbols, learned socio-cultural behavior, or even values more susceptible to change and disguise. Accordingly, there are some groups (and individuals or segments within these groups) that are more assimilable than others, based on the nature or degree of their visibility and their ability or willingness to modify or disguise certain aspects of it. Thus there tends to be a "pecking order" in the successful approximation by each ethnic group of the ideal somatic image held by the majority of the society.

Societies which are dominated by an ethnocentric ethos or racist ideologies are inclined to demand cultural or ethnic homogeneity, and to mete out social penalties for groups who vary or deviate from the normative values. Those minorities, especially stranger groups, which by ascription or volition present the most noticeably visible distinctions, tend to be deemed the most objectionable or threatening to the dominant groups of such societies and the established social order.

To be sure, power, privilege, prestige, wealth, valued technical resources, historicity of presence, and circumstance of entry may offset rejection and maltreatment. However, a minority or stranger group's visibility may affect the perception of a racially predisposed majority to such a negative point that the minority comes to be regarded as incapable or dispossessed of attributes held in esteem by the majority (bias). A highly visible minority group may even be deprived of opportunity to attain these attributes (discrimination). Finally, its visibility may be used as justification for both bias and discrimination against its members (racism).

Different views of American society have led to a number of sociohistorical theses which attempt to explain or predict ethnic stratification and social distance in the United States. A very common underlying aspect among the classical theories refers to the prevailing assimilationist ethos in American society. Gordon (1964) classifies three theories of assimilation: (1) Anglo-conformity; (2) melting pot; and (3) cultural pluralism. All three assume an eventual level of integration of ethnic groups. However, while the first two seem targeted to eventual absorption and invisibility of ethnic minorities as entities, the last assumes their continued existence as groups, but with assimilation on the personal and cultural levels. That is, while the society may be characterized as culturally plural, ethnic groups will participate in a social structure marked by the ethnic integration of secondary and public institutions—thus social assimilation will stand beside cultural pluralism. Sociologists Van der Gerghe (1967) and Blauner (1972) have explicitly refuted the applicability of the immigrant model to American blacks. They stress conflict, discrimination and segregation, rather than assimilation, as the principal characteristic of the experience of black people in this country.

History indicates the exclusiveness and inadequacies in the assimilating mechanisms of the society, particularly as they relate to visible ethnic groups. In fact, the so-called "white backlash" and the more recent reemergence of ethnic activism suggest that the assumed melting of the less visible groups was not as thorough as often assumed. Insofar as ethnic relations go, then, the cultural-plural model may be more adequate to the extent that it describes the American society as comprised of ethnic and cultural groups not fully assimilated and often seeking to retain separate identities, cultural particularities, and functional space.

History also suggests a strong ethnocentric or racist bias among dominant groups in American society. Not only is there an underlying persistent objection to the presence and progress of visible minorities, but also not-quite-invisible or fully-acculturated sections of the majority groups have suffered some degree of suppression and discrimination as well. There is no theoretically successful way to obscure the ethnic competition and racial conflict that exists in the society. Targets, modes of expression, and degree of saliency fluctuate, but the basic ethos continues to be marked by inequality and disfavor toward the visible, in much the same way as other deviant or marginal groups are treated. Such inequality and disfavor, however, tend to be crystallized into or combined with political and economic arrangements. Thus ethnic problems become fused with those of class formation, mobility, stratification, conflict, and struggle—as well as complicating the points of tension and nature of social problems in U.S. society. Therefore, in one sense, visibility constitutes a confounding or intervening variable in the ethnic history of the United States. In a broader sense, it is a crucial stratificational complement in a set of considerations by which groups are hierarchically located and allowed (or disallowed) into the mainstream of power, wealth and prestige of the society.

Consequently, the visibility of the new immigrants presents a serious challenge to the United States, its resident majority, minority groups, government, and other national institutions. The continued present increase and expansion of the new immigrant groups hold serious implications for the future of cultural tone, public affairs, and human relations in the society. Its traditional stance on ethnicity and culture will be further challenged, and agitation by groups demanding greater equality and change in that tradition is likely to recur with greater force in the future unless that stance is boldly reexamined and reevaluated at this point in time.

Changing Ethnic Configurations

In comparing the leading ten source countries in the pre- and post-act periods, certain inferences may be drawn concerning the visibility of the population in terms of how their phenotypical features, language, and culture compare with the present majority United States population (see table 1, p. 77). Such a comparison suggests five broad categories of immigrant populations: Group I, English-speaking Anglo-Saxon; Group II, non-English-speaking European; Group III, Mediterranean and Southern non-English-speaking European; Group IV, Asian; and Group V, West Indian and Latin American. From the pre-act period the top ten source countries of legal immigrants can be categorized as follows: Group I, Canada, United Kingdom, and Ireland (792,932 persons); Group II, Germany, Poland, Hungary, and the Netherlands (561,313 persons); Group III, Italy (255,168 persons); Group IV, none; and Group V, Mexico and Cuba (677,049 persons). In the post-act period there were noticeable changes in the ethnic configuration of legal immigrants. In Group I Ireland dropped out, and the number of immigrants from Canada and the United Kingdom numbered only 392,132 persons; Group II was not represented at all; Group III was represented only by Italy, but by a slightly less volume of 240,358; Group IV showed a diametric change from no representation to the appearance of the Philippines, Korea, and China with a total of 768,938 persons; and Group V almost doubled its volume (1,545,381 persons) as Cuba and Mexico were now accompanied by Jamaica and the Dominican Republic. The point is clear that the new immigrants tend to be characterized by their increased visibility and for reasons transcending recency of arrival. In fact, when borderline cases such as Greece, but more so India, Vietnam, Guyana, Indochina, Haiti, Cuba, and the purported illegals from non-European countries are considered, it is clear that immigration policies and patterns will have a serious impact on the United States as a society.

(See TABLE 1, page 77.)

TABLE 1

Visibility of the Ten Top Source Countries (1953-1965 and 1966-1978)

Pre-act (1953-1965)

Group I		Group II		Group III	Group IV	Group V	
Anglo-Saxon (English Speaking)		European (Non-English Speaking)		Mediterranean and Southern European (Non-English Speaking)	Asian (English and Non-English Speaking)	West Indian and Latin American (English and Non-English Speaking)	
Canada	400,795	Germany	339,605	Italy 255,168	Non-Existent	Cuba	150,597
United Kingdom	305,252	Poland	101,564			Mexico	526,452
Ireland	86,885	Hungary	60,748				
		Netherlands	59,396				
Total	792,932	Total	561,313			Total	677,059

Post-act (1966-1979)

Group I		Group II	Group III	Group IV		Group V	
Canada	196,834	Non-Existent	Italy 196,834...				

Group I		Group II	Group III	Group IV		Group V	
Canada	196,834	Non-Existent	Italy	Philippines	352,528	Cuba	479,459
United Kingdom	195,298		240,358	Korea	229,119	Mexico	732,575
				China	187,291	Jamaica	163,913
						Dominican Republic	169,434
Total	392,132			Total	768,938	Total	1,545,381

Figures based on INS data 1953-1978

One implication of the data being discussed here is the growing possibility of a very important trend—the changing and expanding of the foreign-born population of the United States. Recent U.S. census figures provide reinforcement for this possibility. Overall in 1970, 83 percent of the population was native-born of native parents. Persons of foreign or mixed parents comprised almost 12 percent of the total population, and foreign-born persons equalled about 4.9 percent. The two latter percentages had been in strong decline since 1920. In 1970 more than 50 percent of that foreign-stock segment was concentrated among three countries of Group I (Canada, United Kingdom, and Germany), Poland of Group II, and Mexico of Group V—the latter being the only source of visible ethnics registered in that category. However, whereas decreases were registered in the foreign-born segments and their children in the American population between 1960 and 1970, the decreases were not uniform among countries of origin. Canada and most European countries (not including Greece) showed decreases; Asia, Mexico, Cuba, and the composite of "other America" showed substantial increases (United States Department of Commerce, 1972, p. 103).

Further, of the eight sources which combine to represent 50 percent of the ethnic identifications registered among the American population of the 1960-1970 decade (United States Department of Commerce, 1973a and 1973b, p. 19), Spanish ethnicity is clearly likely to be increased; Italian, English, and German may be reinforced by immigration. Other presently leading ethnicities such as Irish, French, Polish, and Russian are likely to be surpassed eventually by legal and other categories of new and more visible immigrants as they establish residence, naturalize, or bear American-born offspring.

Finally, in terms of language, 79 percent of the U.S. population declared English as its mother tongue according to 1970 census figures. English, therefore, was the leading mother tongue among persons of native, foreign, or mixed parents, and a close second to Spanish as mother tongue among the foreign-born. Other languages ranking high among the top ten as mother tongues of the general population were French, German, Italian, Polish, Yiddish, Swedish, Norwegian, and Slovak. Thus, based on post-act immigration patterns, it is likely that increases or reinforcement would be observed especially among foreign-born and younger natives with foreign or a mixed parent subpopulation in English, Spanish, Italian, and perhaps Chinese. All the other languages are likely to show decreases. It could be that new Asian languages will be detailed. Exceptions on the regional or local level, where focused immigration, traditional ethnic concentration on customs, and special policies and programs serve to institutionalize the use of specific foreign languages as instrumental requirements or traditional devices, can be expected.[4]

There are other areas of the new immigration that have serious policy implications. These include: (1) distribution or secondary movements and the challenges posed for local governance or business; (2) role in the job market and its complications for ethnic politics; (3) family size or growth rate and its implications for population growth and other social services; (4) variations in culture, aspirations, and mass media; and (5) administrative linkages and identities, and implications for diplomacy and international relations. Some of these have developed into salient public issues with the probability of explosive confrontations between new immigrants and the police as well as other social control agencies, native-born ethnic peers, or in the case of immigrants from U.S. territories, with the native majority or nationalist sectors of it. On the other side of the ledger, the phenomenon of new immigration has provided some indication of positive contributions and reconciliations among new immigrants, and between new and old ethnics and their host communities. There is, therefore, urgent need for social scientific study of these aspects of the new immigration with its various nuances as phenomenon and as public issue.

Cities and Colonies: Internationalization of Ethnicity

The new immigrants everywhere, but particularly in cities of their concentration such as New York, dramatize the growing necessity for the conscious interlinking of local, national, international (and global) policies. In New York City, for example, as their presence becomes more consequential, it suggests that the city extends beyond definitions distinguishing it in form and function from countryside or suburb. New York must be seen as a major point of international convergence of labor and capital, and also of exchange of culture, art, academic thought, folklore, ideology, identity, religion, life styles, and technological or technical methods. With regard to the Caribbean immigrants, it may well be that New York City is a northern frontier, or at least a pole in a circular migratory stream not only of bodies but of their objectives, ideas, and sentiments as well. There are signs that New York functions as a site of linkages and of significant cultural and political contacts in which there occurs a coalescence, structural reformation, and fusion of immigrant peoples of various persuasions, cultures, classes, countries, and subregions who were separate, antagonistic, or even ignorant of each other at home.

For example, a pan-Caribbean spirit is emerging in New York City, Washington, D.C., many other Eastern seaboard cities and also in Los

Angeles and Miami. The emergence of even broader cross-identifica-
tion can be observed in the celebration of the West Indian Carnival
and *Dia de la Raza* (Columbus Day) as well as the institution of Caribbean Studies programs, proliferation of Third World radio programs
and stations, and political philosophizing in Eastern cities. Whether
samba or *salsa, shango* or *soucouyant, sancocho* or *souse, sankey* or
son, susu or *sans, sese* or *sa-u-dila,* Afro-Caribbean sounds, terms,
and traits abound in these cities.

The late Ira Reid, a black sociologist and author of the classic *The
Negro Immigrant,* points out that while many black immigrants settled in Chicago and several other Northeastern cities, by 1930 New
York City was already hosting 60 percent of that subpopulation. Even
so, Caribbean immigration cannot be seen as totally different from all
other immigrations into this country. It shares traits with other urban-
oriented or -confined groups such as Jews, Irish, and Italians. Within
the cities themselves, its members also have much in common with the
visible native-born minorities of this country.

It is in the cities, therefore, that one has felt and can still feel the
greatest impact of the Afro-Caribbean and now the Latin American
migrations. It is there that one can observe the struggles, sufferings,
rivalries, and restructuring of the new immigrants among themselves.
It is in the cities that one can best appreciate their cultures, culture-
making and culture-mixing. Cities are the setting of the Caribbean
overseas communities, the stage of Afro-Caribbean immigrant culture.
There are signs that these cities do not serve simply as outposts or
melting pots, but that they are sites of significant social, economic, and
cultural contacts of Caribbean peoples with majority and minority
North American traditions, technology, and treatment. They are also
the settings for interesting coalescence, structural reformations, and
fusion of Caribbean peoples of varying identities, politics, religions,
language groups, subcultures, classes, and sub-regions. For peoples
who were apart, antagonists, and even unaware of each other back
home, these cities have become the scenes of intense interaction,
reidentification, and cross-fertilization among Afro-Caribbean and/or
Latin American cultures.

The city of Miami, Florida, has become rather distinctive from
other American cities by virtue of the saliency of Latin American culture in its various ranks of life. It has been a traditional entrepot and
temporary place of refuge for Caribbean peoples. It serves as host of
the most developed Cuban enclave in the United States. Much of its
older black population is of Bahamian background; more recent refugees come from Cuba, Haiti and Jamaica. The concentration of
Cubans following the Castro takeover, and the presence of a large

number of other Latin American emigres, have combined to make Spanish a functional and compulsory language in Miami, converting Dade County schools into a bilingual-multicultural educational system and creating openings for native-born Latin Americans in local government, and for professionals, businessmen, and firms in the commercial structure of the city. Another result has been the selection of the first Puerto Rican mayor in a mainland city. Additionally, the older Miami-based Cuban-Americans played very active roles in the politics of the Nixon government and Watergate. They voted heavily in favor of the Republican Party and for Ronald Reagan for president of the United States (as they are believed to have done in the first Statehood Party victory in Puerto Rico).

On the international level, the city of Miami has served as an arena of pro- and anti-Castro confrontations, sometimes reaching violent proportions. It has been the base for not only pro-American and anti-Castro broadcasts and incursions, but for visits to Cuba by those members of the "comunidad," responding to the relaxation of travel arrangements between the United States and Cuba.

Political and terrorist groups among the older Cuban refugees represent an important restraining factor in the U.S. government's attitudes toward reconciliation with the Castro government as well as with other radical and progressive leftist or populist governments of Latin America and the Caribbean. Indeed, Miami represents a very dramatic example of the emerging transnational linkage of peoples, institutions, and ideologies, rather than the formal governmental structures that one observes in the lesser circum-Caribbean regions. Miami also emphasizes the strain between the stability sought by states of the region—at the cost of inequality of development, living standards, opportunities, rights, and power within and among them—and the movement of peoples within and even outside the region in search of these equalities.

Using the Cubans as an example, Miami sheds some insights on the conflicts and competitions which a privileged and relatively more powerful and consolidated community can present for the mobile but less organized, endowed, or favored immigrants or native minorities of a city. The colony of Puerto Rico elucidates the same, only this time vis-à-vis a native majority subject population. In both places, Cuban refugees preempted, displaced, and frustrated the political and economic aspirations of the native population. It is a generally accepted fact that this particular immigrant population played a significant role in the campaigning and election of the island's first statehood governor, Luis A. Ferre, and in the power and prominence that the statehood parties now exercise in Puerto Rican politics. As in Miami, Cuban ref-

ugees and their children with American citizenship have become beneficiaries of the federal structure and programs directed to Puerto Rico.
Insofar as they share Hispanic background with their host society, the
expressions of conflicts and competition are more explicated in economic, political, and sometimes racial terms. Comparable to Miami,
Puerto Rico is now designated by federal decree to be the recipient of a
proportion of the new black Cuban and Haitian immigrants without
previous consultation with the local government, despite popular opposition and with no indication of that preference by the refugees
themselves.[5] Corresponding imbalances and somewhat similar tensions have been registered in the U.S. Virgin Islands with regard to the
overseas American community and West Indian labor forces, and in
Guam and other U.S.-administered Pacific Island territories concerning Asian refugees and immigrant investors. By changing the details of
cultural requirements, these refugees have been increasing their political influence as well.

The recent violence in Miami cannot be divorced from the Cuban
presence or their involvement as precipitators or victims. Neither can
the recent eruptions in Cuba, Jamaica, and Haiti be isolated from the
concentration and active presence in Miami of older politicized refu-
gee or immigrant groups from these respective islands, nor from U.S.
foreign relations or business ties with government and private interests of these islands.

Contrary to the antagonistic position espoused by the image-mak-
ers and issue-persuaders of immigration as the cause of the plethora of
social problems facing the nation, the scholarly analytical approach
posits immigration as an index to and consequence of the complex in-
terconnected national and international inequalities we face in today's
world. Immigrants often leave from local situations of restricted rights
and societies of limited resources or opportunities in search of equality, improved life chances, and the promise of the "good life" they have
heard about. Generally, as aliens—especially if illegal and/or highly
"visible"—they are prone to face other forms of inequality and hostility in their new host society. Without much defense, they must com-
pete and later coalesce and be associated with the native-born working
classes and minority groups who are suffering similar conditions of inequality. Usually the places in which immigrants resettle—communities, cities, and colonies—are not empowered for self-government or
foreign relations policies. These places share less than equally in the
power to make appropriate decisions concerning immigration.

In the final analysis, neither inequality nor immigration is an isolated matter; many of the problems each poses and the people who
must endure these problems must be assessed within frameworks

other than those contained in the isolationist model. Contrary to the stereotype, new immigrants are not villainous parasites encroaching upon the decreasing resources and space in the United States, but are, instead, peoples whose countries contribute to the U.S.'s continued development and whose culture, competency, and commitment are important elements of the social dynamics of this society. They are also agents in the internationalization of ethnicity.

The rise in saliency of the new immigration itself as a public issue has been slow and erratic. For more than five years after the passage of the 1965 act, the new immigration as a phenomenon was the concern of a rather small group of people. As such, both immigration and immigrants suffered a Ralph Ellison-like invisibility relative to more salient international and domestic issues. Even within the academic enterprise, immigration and immigrants had lost their traditional places of priority as topics for research, writing, and study. Indeed, there were a few classical social science works produced, i.e., Mill's *Puerto Rican Journey,* Reid's *The Negro Immigrants,* and Gamio's *Mexican Immigration,* but for all practical purposes immigration and immigrants had become the specializations of historians and geographers, as if they were fixed or natural things of the past. American political scientists studied political behavior of established ethnics but not of *new* immigrants, while the attention of most sociologists, economists, and anthropologists was drawn to other public issues and social problems. Further, none of these scholarly groups showed awareness of the relationship of their topics of study to the new immigration or immigrants.

The immediate impact of all this was a lull in the study of immigration, immigrants, or even immigration policy (Bryce-Laporte, 1979). The larger results took the form of serious gaps in our knowledge of immigration, related processes and problems, characteristics beyond journalistic and demographic details of immigrants, their host settings or societies, and variations in the causes and conditions of departure and reception. Much of the details of immigrants' everyday living and the meaning of their migration remained unregistered beyond cursory government data; so too the significance and tensions of their presence went for the most part unscrutinized. Much of the earlier phase of the new immigration, therefore, took place in a vacuum of knowledge, theory, method, data and expertise.

The new immigration also suffered an image of underestimated, confused, and distorted importance. It was a movement caught in an unequal struggle among unequal antagonists and advocates, in the confusion of advocacy with analysis, and the abdication by academics of their traditional responsibilities. Among those filling the void created by the abandonment of the study of immigration by legitimate scholars were the anti-immigration campaigners. Some of these persons and groups have had genuine, if misguided, misgivings about the new immigration or some aspects or consequences of it. Others responded to it opportunistically or in a blind, reactionary fashion. Their tactics varied from blatant racist, nativist, and isolationist propaganda to more sophisticated utilization of the image, jargon, paraphernalia, and personnel of the social sciences and public media to persuade the public, policy-makers, and funding agencies about the legitimacy of their cause, the urgency of their contentions, the adequacy of their method of analysis, and such proposals for solutions as "Cease immigration," "Close the borders," "Expel the illegals," and "Zero population growth or doom"

Scholars, particularly social scientists, cannot be absolved either. Some naively or consciously cooperated not only as citizens but as experts (even minority group scholars) with the perpetrators of these activities; others themselves exploited the theme of immigration and the focus and situations of the immigrants, their host societies, and local rivals as long as it provided career mobility, notoriety, or finance for research. Hence on one level the nation witnessed raids, blatant brutalities, and civil rights abuses against immigrants, and on the other malicious distortions of numbers, scenarios, and claims against the new immigrants. Their presence was termed the root of all evils. Their expulsion was to be the solution to all problems.

Generally, coming from systems or milieux of inequality, new immigrants tend to be the most vulnerable, exploitable, and defenseless group in society. Politically and linguistically timid, they are disinclined to take the risk of confrontation even in their own defense. Economically insecure, strangers to a new ambience, they tend to be collectively passive or cautious regarding their status. This is particularly true of illegals who allegedly abound in the latest immigration wave, and also of parolees, students, and dependents of dubious or temporary status. Even legal immigrants upon arrival do not have immediate access to control agencies for communal action or politicking in their own self-defense. Thus opportunistic politicians and desperate publics often find immigrants to be convenient targets for their hostilities and harassment.

Ironically, legal immigrants are presented less as a public issue than the illegal ones, and they suffer almost equally from the bad press directed toward their illegal peers. They benefit less from public sympathy than refugees who are at least newsworthy at the outset and for some time may be advantageously presented as public issues. It may well be that the new immigrants of today are much less beneficiaries of sympathetic mediation from social scientists or from successful ethnic peers or predecessors than the waves of European-dominated immigration of the recent past. This is unfortunate, given the origin of American sociology, its rootedness in the concern with urban immigrants and the tradition of the Chicago School, which provided us with some of the major early classics on empirical research, social theory, and criticism on social problems such as immigration, ethnicity, and urbanism.

Today we find ourselves in the lamentably counter-productive situation where advocacy is increasingly mistaken or allowed to precede analysis in the determination of policy. Thus often the analysis is directed to issues or to a distorted picture of the phenomenon, rather than to the phenomenon itself. Policy also emerges from a reaction to issues and images and not to the phenomenon itself, creating avoidable secondary problems and half-answers. Research is often called upon not to yield truth or provide guidance, but to camouflage advocacy or ideology and to legitimize policy arrived at on purely political or economic grounds. This is a double bind in immigration studies. The making of immigration into a political issue is dispensable for the improvement of immigration data and their value to science; it undermines that value through the political misuse of data and research (Couch, 1979). One solution to the bind is not to abandon the field, not to succumb to the temptations. A greater solution must entail our persistence as academic researchers in being critical of imposters, reflexive toward our professional peers, and diligent in carrying out both our academic and political imperatives in a fair, efficient, and daring manner toward the greater good of humanity (Bryce-Laporte, 1979).

Overall, the presence of new immigrants will likely add emphasis to the tensions between two historic American traditions: (1) the myth of open reception and equal opportunity for all peoples who come to this country in search of freedom, progress and security; and (2) the difficulties of acceptance and inequality of opportunities (and rewards) experienced by peoples of pronounced ethnic-cultural visibilities in the United States. Today the myth is being taunted through the practices of entry and control regulations by consular, immigration, and labor officials, border and police authorities, and the vociferous campaigns of panic by journalistic and special interest sources regarding overpopulation, illegal aliens, and welfare and work competition. The reality, on the other hand, exists with no recent clear-cut hint of solution from either the government, the academy, or the general public. Positive reactions to civil rights acts and affirmative action programs have not been easily forthcoming, not even in the educational sector. Generally the most open, benign, and initial stepping stone toward realizing the American Dream for immigrants, the urban public school has become in recent years the arena of heightened contact and bitter confrontations between traditionally visible and invisible ethnics on various levels. In part, the problem is one of increasing opportunities of entry and competition without commensurate increases in resources or quality of accommodation and reward. On another level, it is the consequence of a mass-level change in the translation of the American Dream (or promise) of equal opportunity for all and a lag or inadequacy of response on policy and institutional levels (Bryce-Laporte, 1977).

Bell (1976), Borgatta (1976), and Parsons (1976) have denounced as a deviation from U.S. norms the recent shift from a demand for individual to group opportunities (or rights) in the public arenas of this nation. The approach which they espoused included biases toward those persons or groups who approximated West European standards of ethics, a Judaeo-Christian culture, and a general Protestant-capitalist-industrial ethos (Ringer, 1976; Forsythe, 1976). It is crucial to observe, therefore, that the shift to a demand for equality for groups as groups emerged from the frustrations suffered by groups who were once kept disenfranchised and deficient in the past precisely because of the distance and nature of their divergence from the traditional normative standards. That shift represents an effort of the disenfranchised to address the persistent dilemma of the United States, both nationally and internationally, between the progress it seeks for itself and the equality it promises to share with its members but has hitherto not fulfilled. In this lies the manner in which immigration as a phenomenon may force policy-makers to confront a larger reality than the esoteric or instrumental interests which normally seem to motivate their actions.

NOTES

[1] This paper was prepared originally for presentation at the Green Bay Colloquium on Ethnicity and Policy, University of Wisconsin American Ethnic Studies Coordinating Committee, May-June 1980. The author wishes to acknowledge the assistance of Ms. Betty Dyson, Mrs. Constance Trombley, Mr. Wil Morris, and Ms. Kimberly Wingfield in completing the paper. Special acknowledgement goes to Ms. Katherine Williams, Mr. Trevor Purcell, Ms. Dorothy Parker, and the staff in the Statistics Section of the INS. The author, however, accepts sole responsibility for this work and whatever shortcomings herein contained. The content of this paper does not reflect policy of the Smithsonian Institution.

[2] See chapters 1 and 2 in *The Tarnished Golden Door, Civil Rights Issues in Immigration,* a report of the United States Commission on Civil Rights (Washington, D.C.: U.S. Government Printing Office, 1980).

[3] Visibility here is used in the Goffman (1963) sense of the word, meaning perceivable obstructiveness of a particular trait to the treatment of its bearers as normal or equal human beings. Invisibility in this context refers to the assumed ordinariness or normalcy of the bearer which results in positive reactions (at least from the viewpoint of the majority group). Invisibility has another use associated with it (Ellison, 1947), which tends to suggest the bearer as being purposefully ignored as if nonexistent because of perceived obstructiveness rather than being overlooked for being so proximate to the normative or somatic ideal of the majority group. This latter kind of invisibility is more akin to that suffered by "forgotten minorities," such as the "white ethnics" and the smaller ethnic contingents which tend to be subsumed under larger, more established visible groupings, e.g., West Indians as blacks, Koreans, Philippines or Samoans as Asian-Americans, and some less established Latin groups as Chicanos or Puerto Ricans (see Baca and Boyan, 1980; Bryce-Laporte, 1968; Domingues, 1973; Pido, 1975; and Whitney, 1972).

The argument for social or cultural visibility as the original *raison d'être* for the severe rejection and discrimination is most pointedly made by historians Jordan, 1968; Degler, 1971; and Dewry, 1964.

[4] In 1980 the U.S. Department of Education issued for the first time directives in support of bilingual education. (See the "Lau Regulations," U.S. Department of Education, 1980.)

[5] New York Times, September 24, 1980

REFERENCES

Baca, Reynaldo and Bryan, Dexter. "Social Invisibility: The Case of the Mexican Undocumented Worker." 1980 (unpublished).

Bell, Daniel. "Ethnicity and Social Change," In *Ethnicity, Theory and Experience,* ed. Nathan Glazer and Daniel P. Moynihan. Cambridge, Mass. Harvard University Press, 1976, pp. 141-76.

Blauner, Robert. *Racial Oppression in America.* New York: Harper and Row, 1972.

Borgatta, Edgar F. "The Concept of Reverse Discrimination and Equality of Opportunity," *American Sociologist,* 11, No. 2. (May 1976): 62-73.

Bryce-Laporte, Roy S. "Black Immigrants: The Experience of Visibility and Inequality." *Journal of Black Studies,* 3, No. 1. (September 1972): 29-56.

_____."Visibility of the New Immigrant," *Society,* 14, No. 6 (September/October 1977), (whole No. 110): 18-22.

_____."The New Immigration: A Challenge to Our Sociological Imagination," In *Sourcebook on the New Immigration,* Ed. R. S. Bryce-Laporte. New Brunswick, N. J.: Transaction Books, 1979, pp. 459-72.

Couch, Stephen R. "Quantitative Immigration Data, Scientific Knowledge and Public Policy: Possibilities, Limitations and Interrelationships," In *Quantitative Data and Immigration Research,* Eds. Stephen R. Couch and Roy S. Bryce-Laporte. Washington, D.C.: Smithsonian Institution, 1979, pp. 259-83.

Degler, Carl N. *Neither Black or White.* New York: The Macmillan Company, 1971.

Department of Education. "Nondiscrimination Under Programs Receiving Federal Financial Assistance Through the Education Department" (The Lau Decision). *Federal Register,* August 5, 1980, Washington, D.C.: U.S. Government Printing Office.

Dewry, Henry. "Slave and the Plantation," In *Black Culture in the United States.* Ed. Rhoda Goldstein. New York: Thomas Crowell Company, 1964.

Dominguez, Virginia. "Spanish-Speaking Caribbeans in New York: 'The Middle Race,'" *Revista Interamericana,* 3 (1973): 135-42.

Ellison, Ralph. *The Invisible Man.* New York: Random House, Inc, 1947.

Forsythe, Dennis. "Black Immigrants and the American Ethos: Thesis and Observations," 1976 (unpublished).

Goffman, Erving. *Stigma.* Englewood Cliffs, N. J.: Prentice-Hall, Inc., 1963.

Gordon, Milton M. *Assimilation in America.* New York: Oxford University Press, 1964.

Jordan, Winthrop. *White Over Black.* Chapel Hill: University of North Carolina Press, 1968.

————."Base in Puerto Rico to House Refugees." *New York Times,* September 24, 1980, pp. A1, A20.

Parsons, Talcott. "Some Theoretical Considerations in the Nature and Trends of Change and Ethnicity." In *Ethnicity, Theory and Experience.* Eds. Nathan Glazer and Daniel P. Moynihan. Cambridge, Mass.: Harvard University Press, 1976, pp. 53-83.

Pido, Antonio. "A Conflict Study of Nonwhite Immigrant Minority: The Case of the Filipinos in a Midwestern United States City" (a dissertation proposal). East Lansing, Mich.: Michigan State University.

Ringer, Benjamin. "Affirmative Action, Quotas and Meritocracy," *Transaction* (January-February 1976).

United States Commission on Civil Rights. The *Tarnished Golden Door: Civil Rights Issues in Immigration.* Washington, D.C.: U.S. Government Printing Office, 1980.

United States Department of Commerce (Census Bureau). "Country of Origin of the Foreign Stock for the United States, 1970 and 1960: (Supplementary Report. *1970 Census of Population,* 1972, pp. 1-3.

Van der Berghe, Pierre. *Race and Racism: A Comparative Perspective.* New York: John Wiley and Sons, 1967.

Whitney, Phillip B. "The Forgotten Minority: The Filipinos in the United States," *Bulletin of Bibliography and Magazine Notes,* 29, No. 3. (July-September 1972): 73-83.

The Political Economy Context of Language in Social Service Delivery for Hispanics[1]

Adalberto Aguirre, Jr.

University of California, Riverside

Hispanics have become the fastest growing minority group in the United States. Optimistic predictions are that the 1980 census will reveal close to 20 million Hispanics residing in the United States. The most recent population report from the Bureau of the Census lists the Hispanic population as being around 12 million, with the majority (7 million) being of Mexican origin.[2] Some of the more salient characteristics of the Hispanic population are the following:[3]

1. The median age for Hispanics is 22 years old compared to a median of 30 years for the non-Hispanic population. Close to 13% of all Hispanic persons are under 5 years of age, and 5% are 65 years or older. Comparative figures for the non-Hispanic population are 7% and 11% respectively.

2. The unemployment rate for Hispanics 16 years and older averages 3 percentage points higher than the white population. 8% of Hispanic persons are employed as professional and technical workers, and 25% are employed as operatives (i.e., garage workers, produce packers, manufacturing checkers, etc.). Comparative figures for the white population are 17% and 15% respectively.

3. The median income for the Hispanic family is $12,600 compared with a median of $17,900 for white families. Income differences are also present by type of Hispanic family: the median income of Puerto Rican families is $8,300; for Cuban families $15,300; and for Mexican families $12,800. In general, the Hispanic household has a median per capita income that is 49% as much as the median for the white household.

4. Hispanic families in rental households are 6 times more likely to
   be overcrowded than white families, while those in owner-occu-
   pied households are 5 times as likely.

5. The high school completion rate for Hispanics is 30% below the
   completion rate for white persons. The college completion rate is
   70% below the completion rate for white persons, and Hispanic
   persons with 4 or more years of college earned 70% of the average of white persons with the same educational attainment.

Despite the persistent domestic problems Hispanics have in housing, education, jobs and health, it is the rapid expansion of this population that is drawing the attention of Washington policy-makers. Hispanics are a growing source of political power, especially in Florida,
California, Texas, and New York; policies affecting Hispanics in the
U.S. may play a vital role in U.S. access to Mexican oil and gas,[4] and
greater Hispanic representation in the Washington bureaucracy may
aid foreign policy with Latin American countries not friendly with the
U.S.

My purpose in this essay is to offer some comments regarding the
political economy issues for the inclusion of the Spanish language in
social services for Hispanics. My principal concern is to raise theoretical issues regarding the effects of a rapidly growing Hispanic population on social service delivery, as well as on the use of such services to
label and control members of the population. Specifically, the concepts
of *rationalization* and *bureaucratization* will be employed to demonstrate how the principal barrier to social service delivery for Hispanics—language problems—may well be employed as an efficient tool for
the demobilization and depolitization of the Hispanic population.[5] In
an essay in political economy, mechanisms of social control are extremely important for understanding the structure of social allocation
models for Hispanics in the United States.

Social Services and the Economy

The introduction of social services by the federal government, especially during the New Deal, was primarily designed to help the poor.
The government intervened for those not able to "hold their own" by
assuming responsibility for their well-being. As a result, social service
programs and their agencies became legitimate actors in U.S. society,
and provided the poor with income, housing, education, and health
care.[6]

It must not be assumed, however, that social services arose primarily as a benevolent response by a capitalistic environment to human

needs, but rather as an environment preparing itself to deal during the Great Depression with a growing number of unemployed and frustrated people. Piven and Cloward[7] describe the growing numbers of dissatisfied unemployed workers during the Depression:

> Many began to define their hardships, not as an individual fate, but as a collective disaster, not as a mark of individual failure, but as a fault of "the system." As the legitimacy of economic arrangements weakened, anger and protest escalated. The Depression thus gave rise to the largest movement of the unemployed in the history of this country.

Similarly, Richard Quinney has observed that one of the most significant results of the Depression was a surplus population of unemployed working-class people.[8] The rapid growth of this population served as a catalyst for the growth of social services and of the welfare system. Growth in social services became a response to specific areas of growth in the unemployed population and resulted in social and political controls over a surplus population. Regarding the political meaning of this surplus population, O'Conner observes:[9]

> Unable to gain employment in the monopoly industries by offering their laborpower at lower than going wage rates. . .and unemployed, underemployed, or employed at low wages in competive industries, the surplus population increasingly became dependent on the state.

In overview then, social services (e.g., the welfare system) facilitated the operation of social controls over a population to appease mass disorder arising from unemployment. As mass unemployment led to outbreaks of turmoil during the Depression, relief programs were initiated and expanded to absorb and control enough of the unemployed to restore order. But as turbulence subsided, the relief system contracted, expelling those who were needed to populate the lower wage labor market.

Keeping in mind the observations made by Gerth and Mills[10] regarding the lack of an independent existence for persons and institutions, we can see that social services became a *rational* means of control for an institution interested in achieving its own goals and not its members'.[11] That is, social services became *rational* in their pursuit for control by placing limits on what an individual can do when confronted with a choice situation. Given the social context (i.e., poverty, unemployment) in which most recipients of social services found themselves, and the cross-current of ideological forces (i.e., individualism), social services became a satisfactory rather than optimal solution for these individuals.[12]

At the same time, social services were also developing an element of bureaucratic control over the individual by satisfying general needs (i.e., income), but not using the recipients' personal needs to define the ends for social service organization. Bureaucratic control came to rest on the social structure and in the interrelationships of social service delivery. As a social process, the limitation of choices for the individual predicates that social services will become a bureaucratic organization controlling the structures for participation and defining the environment for participation. Analogous to the development of bureaucratic control in social services, Richard Edwards[13] outlines how bureaucratic control developed in the large firm at the turn of the nineteenth century:

> Large firms developed methods of organization that are more formalized and more consciously contrived than simple control; they are "structured" forms of control. Two possibilities existed: more formal, consciously contrived controls could be embedded in either the physical structure of the labor process (producing technical control) or in its social structure (producing "bureaucratic" control). In time, employers used both, for they found that the new systems made control more institutional and hence less visible to workers. . . .

In short, social services are rational in that they limit individuals to choices present only within the supportive structures (or the environment), and bureaucratic in that recipients believe that the organization of these services is done with their end in mind.[14]

Specific Issues

Given our rather limited view of social services in the U.S. and the lack of a fully developed theory of social services, by examining the political context of economic dependence on social services we can outline two issues within the social services area that have implications for the Hispanic population.

Real Income

In the welfare state, social service spending is legitimated by policymakers as necessary to increase the real income of the working poor. The structural condition of the working poor as peripheral participants in a capitalistic working economy implies that increases in their standard of living will not arise from a demand for higher wages, but from the number of social services they receive. Social services thus become an effective mechanism for suppressing the need to push for higher wages.

Another way of approaching the issue is to observe again that social services were introduced to help the working poor and, perhaps more importantly, to maintain cohesion and reproduction of social structure among them. In practical terms, the originators were determined to keep the working poor productive by teaching them how to read and write and remain free from disease. As such, the availability and receipt of social services were seen as increasing the real income of the working poor by keeping them active in the labor force.

Employers recognize that too low a level of wages will diminish the worker's physical capacity, and that too low a level of social services will undermine the rudiments of social structure. Minimal service levels, therefore, become a goal—minimal social service support fosters a steady stream of workers who are desperate for jobs, even low paying ones. The availability of these services also weakens the bargaining power of the working poor and absorbs their labor when it is not needed. Thus a dependency relationship is established that effectively cripples social action; people on welfare do not go on strike against the welfare system, or against anything else for that matter.

Private corporations have neither been ignorant of the political uses of social services nor unwilling to use them as control mechanisms over employees. For example, Richard Edwards[15] argues that welfare capitalism in private industry arose out of an interest to create in workers a sense of loyalty. However, implicit in the concern for providing employees with social services was the belief that the public would perceive them as being responsible to and caring of their workers. Edward summarizes the issues as follows:

> Welfare capitalism, then, represented a sophisticated, well-financed, and widely implemented plan for controlling labor. It reflected the large capitalists' awareness of the need for positive incentives in hierarchial control in order to attract workers' sympathies. It provided considerable tangible benefits to those who submitted to the company's paternalism, and it especially rewarded those who over long periods refrained from union activity and remained "loyal" to the firm.

It appears then that regardless of whether social services were located in the public or private sector, the dominant ideology was one of bureaucratic control and rationalization of individual behavior.

Labor Pool

Just as the expansion of social services was designed to meet the needs of the working poor, reduction of these services increased the size of the low-wage labor pool and thus benefited corporate interests. For example, high levels of social service spending permit individuals to stay off the labor market for relatively long periods of time as they look for either better jobs or non-work roles. In addition, high welfare payments allow poor mothers to stay at home when their children are still infants, and unemployment insurance allows workers to wait to be called back to their old jobs. However, restriction of these social services forces recipients to become less calculative in their social activities and willing to accept whatever employment they can get.

Hispanics and Social Services

Not only were growing numbers of Anglo U.S. citizens finding themselves unemployed and on welfare rolls during the Great Depression, but Mexican farm laborers, displaced by Anglo-Americans desperate for work, were being forced to migrate to the cities, hoping either to find work or obtain money through the relief (welfare) program. The growing members of Mexicans in urban areas quickly aroused concern among Anglo citizens regarding the cost of welfare, and quickly brought about the observation that Mexicans were also taking jobs away from Anglos. Consequently, the general feeling developed that foreigners were responsible for unemployment and that they should be returned to their homeland. It was also widely believed that the Anglo-American taxpayer would save money by shipping Mexicans home.[16]

Though techniques for deporting Mexicans varied from city to city, the general movement was inspired by Herbert Hoover's favorite excuse for the state of the economy—that widespread unemployment was caused by the large number of illegal aliens in the U.S. For example, Hoover's Secretary of Labor, William N. Doak, estimated that 400,000 aliens had evaded the immigration laws and that at least one-fourth of these were readily deportable—the majority being Mexicans.[17] Armed with figures like these, Doak requested that Congress appropriate funds for the deportation of illegals and that $500,000 be authorized immediately for the expansion of the Border Patrol. Following the lead of the federal government, local authorities throughout the Southwest and Midwest began initiating bills that would prohibit illegal aliens from engaging in business or seeking employment. In addition, local authorities went one step further by making documented immigrants subject to the same bills.[18]

It was probably the large number of Mexicans on relief that prompted the Border Patrol to use welfare programs as the primary arena for locating deportable Mexicans. In the end this permitted the social service bureaucracy to manipulate a population of individuals to avoid potential conflict within the Anglo-American population, and to provide the symbolic apparatus through which the federal government would appear to be dealing with the central causes of the Depression. The observation among some researchers that Los Angeles was the model repatriating city will permit us to focus on that city to examine the role of social welfare services in the deportation of Mexicans.[19]

Los Angeles city officials devised programs, with the joint cooperation of charity organizations and the California Department of Unemployment, to encourage Mexicans to return home. When a Mexican approached these departments for assistance, a case worker would be assigned to that family. It was the case worker's sole responsibility to persuade the head of the family that they would be happier in Mexico. If they agreed to return, fare and subsistence to the border would be paid for the entire family. Should more persuasion be needed, local authorities would bring in the Mexican consul for assistance. Abraham Hoffman[20] summarizes the situation in Los Angeles:

> Mexican families living on county relief were particularly susceptible to suggestions of repatriation for a variety of reasons. There was little likelihood of employment as the economic depression progressively worsened. The offer from the board of supervisors' charities and public welfare committee contained a number of inducements, which were increased when the number of volunteers of repatriation declined. Such benefits as free transportation, food, clothing, medical aid, and the assurance of cooperation by the Mexican government and railroads, all presented strong temptation to accept repatriation. Plans for repatriation colonies in Mexico were constantly being projected and there were hints, accurate or not, that a return to the United States would be possible after an improvement in economic conditions.

Similarly, in Detroit social workers used other subtle measures to persuade the prospective returnee. During the winter Mexican families on relief were placed on a cafeteria list, forcing them to eat at a local mess hall where they were purposefully served unfamiliar foods such as sauerkraut instead of the traditional beans.[21] Along with threats that the rent would not be paid or welfare payments cut, social workers continually reminded the Mexicans that they would not only be happier in Mexico but that they would also be eating healthier and familiar foods.[22]

Current Problematic Issues

Perhaps the two most often-cited problem areas in the delivery of social services to Hispanics are the language problems encountered by limited English speaking Hispanics receiving notification of service program cuts only in English,[23] and the unavailability of bilingual staff or appropriate staff necessary when dealing with language minority persons.[24] Below, two studies are reviewed that examine how the lack of appropriate language resources and bilingual staff places the Hispanic recipient of social and public services at the mercy of the institution.

The Mendoza Report[25] examines the extent to which Hispanic clients suffer language-related costs and/or delays in their pursuit of benefits and services from the New York City Department of Social Services (NYCDSS). A total of 1,112 Hispanic recipients of public assistance were interviewed in their homes by teams of bilingual interviewers between September 1977 and January 1978. Briefly, the principal findings were as follows:

1. 10.2% of limited English speaking ability (LESA) clients reported being denied access to the welfare center because of their inability to communicate their problems clearly to English speaking receptionists. A large majority (89.3%) of LESA clients reported that they were unable to understand their application forms in English. 10.9% of LESA clients seeking assistance in filling out their applications also reported that their applications were delayed because the translator or interpreter did not fill them out correctly. 12.8% of LESA clients reported that their inability to get a translator influenced their decision not to go to the welfare center.

2. On the average, LESA clients spent $5.00 per visit to the welfare center for interpreter services. LESA clients exclusively spent a conservatively estimated $810 per year for interpretation services when they attempted to communicate with the NYCDSS.

3. Non-monetary services and benefits which are normally available to Department of Social Services clients were not often accessible to LESA clients due to the inability of the NYCDSS to provide information about these services in the language understood by the LESA client. 9% of LESA clients reported having been denied access to non-monetary services because they were not able to communicate with the welfare worker.

4. LESA clients (47.5%) reported that they had to take a minor to serve as an interpreter in the welfare center. Of these, 77.8% re-

ported that their children missed from one to five days of school per year for this program.

5. LESA clients (50.8%) reported having had to continue conversations with welfare workers in English, even though they could neither express themselves in nor understand English. Of the remaining LESA clients, 42.5% were told to return to the welfare office with an interpreter.

6. The data clearly showed that the rights of privacy of Hispanic LESA clients were continually violated. The majority (78.4%) of LESA clients reported having to bring someone with them to the welfare center to help them because of language difficulties, thus involving a third party in discussions of a confidential and intimate nature. An extremely high proportion (89.3%) of LESA clients reported involving a third party in filling out their application forms.

Similarly, a study was undertaken by the California Department of Health Services in response to complaints from the Hispanic community regarding emergency bilingual health services at San Francisco General Hospital.[26] Investigators from the state Civil Rights Office were assigned to the hospital on a twenty-four hour basis for three weeks. Out of a reported 38,440 contacts by the public, 4,804 or 12.5% were made by monolingual Spanish speaking persons. At the time, only 7% of the staff in public contact positions could speak Spanish. Principal findings were as follows:

1. All of the seven emergency units available were found to have services accessible to only English speaking patients. Two of the six emergency units had no Spanish speaking personnel on the day shift, and three of the emergency units had no Spanish speaking personnel on the night shift.

2. In psychiatric emergency, a twenty-four hour unit with three shifts, none of the nineteen people on the day shift, none of the thirteen people on the evening shift, and only one of the fourteen people on the night shift could speak Spanish.

3. In emergency admitting, only one of the twenty-seven people on these shifts could speak Spanish, even though 21% of all contacts these employees had with the public were with people who speak only Spanish.

4. Investigators witnessed hospital employees in the emergency area trying to communicate in English and in hand gestures with monolingual Spanish speaking persons.

Policy Implications

C. Wright Mills[27] identifies three roles for the social scientist in the public sphere: philosopher-king (the social scientist occupies a position of power and is also extraordinarily knowledgeable); independent philosopher ("It is to remain independent, to do one's own work, to select one's own problems, but to direct this work at kings as well as to 'publics'."); and advisor to the king (the social scientist as technician who provides information to others, usually bureaucratic officials). I have long believed that the Hispanic scholar must wear two hats and always promote collaborative social research between kings and publics. His fellow social scientists, as kings in a kingdom of their own, must be educated regarding the characteristics of the Hispanic community, and the Hispanic community must also be educated regarding the changing ideologies of Anglo-American institutions. For this reason, statements presented in the following pages will be speculative ones, and will be the product of a social scientist in the role of "independent philosopher."

Perhaps one way of adding some coherency to our previous comments regarding the political economy of social services is by simplifying the obvious in general observational statements:

1. The socio-economic political context has been shown to have a definite effect on public policy decisions. The use of social services during the Great Depression was a bureaucratic response to a potential political crisis arising from the growing dissatisfaction of unemployed workers and the economic necessity to "save" workers for future low wage work. Accordingly, the use of social services during the Depression as a major recruiting center for deportees by the Border Patrol was a rational policy response to a larger bureaucratic need in the federal government to appear active against an eroding economic environment.

2. The lack of adequate language services and bilingual personnel in social and public service agencies currently restricts the participation of limited English speaking Hispanics. Programs become inaccessible, communication with social workers is distorted, costs are incurred by the individual in dealings with the agency—all resulting in frustration, an inadequate quality of life, and a decision not to seek needed services. In the long run, these may be crucial qualitative issues responsible for fostering the fatalistic attitude among Hispanics in their dealings with Anglo-American institutions.

It would appear from the latter observation (2) that the addition of appropriate language resources and adequate staff would increase the effectiveness and scope of social service delivery to the Hispanic population. This certainly appears to be a logical conclusion, but is it a rational one? Following the argument of Toussaint Hocevar,[28] it would not be rational for the social service bureaucracy for the following reasons:

1. The majority (e.g., Anglo-American) client would be affected by the mere fact that the minority client is being supplied with minority-specific, rather than majority-specific, public goods. That is, the availability of services in Spanish would communicate a *qualitative* difference in services to the majority client and a growing suspicion that he is receiving less (e.g., real income vis-à-vis services) at the expense of the minority client. As long as services in Spanish are not available for Hispanics, the majority client is willing to believe that minorities are getting less while he is getting more. (This, of course, becomes a reflection of the social inequality present between Anglo-Americans and Hispanics in the U.S.

   However, once services become available in Spanish, differentials are leveled off, and both Hispanics and Anglos are subject to the same social services. As a result, Anglo-American clients come to believe that equality in services (i.e., vis-à-vis the use of Spanish) is brought about by making it a cost to them (e.g., in the form of eliminating differentials in service delivery).

2. Adequate communication from the use of appropriate language services with Hispanic clients would lead to the creation of a linguistically neutral environment within the social service bureaucracy. Given that the extent to which public goods meet individual preferences is dependent upon political processes, a linguistically neutral environment has the potential of permitting the development of a political structure that takes minority preferences into account. This latter point becomes interesting when one considers the rapid growth of the Hispanic population in the United States.

On the other hand, the use of appropriate staff would be a rational decision for the social service bureaucracy because it might serve as a further limitation on the accessibility of services. I believe we have been deceived in believing that the addition of bilingual personnel in social service agencies would benefit Hispanic clients. If our experiences with bilingual education programs in this country have taught us anything, it is that schools and school districts are supportive of their bilingual personnel only to the extent that they adhere to the dominant educational ideologies—the principal one being the sociolinguistic assimilation of language minority children.[29] We would expect, as a result, the social service bureaucracy to recruit staff for the handling of language minority clients that are supportive of the larger bureaucratic goal. Thus the decision would be rational in that bureaucratic control would be expressed through this organizational linkage—Hispanic clients would be led to believe they were receiving more while actually getting less. A nice Catch-22 situation for the Hispanic client.

In regard to the first conclusion (1) above, it is extremely unlikely, given the growing importance of Mexico as an oil-producing country, that the United States would use the social service bureaucracy to victimize Mexicans. It is much more likely that an attitude of tolerance will develop. The increasing number of Cubans being taken in by the U.S. symbolically reinforces an increasing attitude of tolerance—not acceptance—toward Hispanics.

The increasing heterogeneity of the Hispanic community may prompt the use of social services as a reward system. Given the fact that social services are subject to political manipulation, it may be both possible and highly rational to use social services to reward that element in the Hispanic population with the weakest political potential. This would lead to factionalism and, most likely, accusations of imperialism from the other elements. It would not be dissimilar to the present conflict between blacks and Hispanics for the distribution of limited federal, state, and local monies—a conflict that is intensified when one considers the claim of census researchers that the Hispanic population will increase in size beyond the black population by the turn of the century.[30] The above prevents the development of a coalition that would have a better chance of influencing the political structure. Accordingly, the use of social services to selectively reward members of the Hispanic population would harm the development of working coalitions and would take away the political force from a population that is increasingly criticized in Washington circles for its homogeneous identity.

I have tried to extend Max Weber's views on the role of bureaucracy in society by describing how an environment is susceptible to bureaucratic manipulation, in that social action is the result of preferences and decision maxims that mirror the institutional socialization of the individual and the institutional character of society.[31] Claus Mueller[32] outlines the issue as follows:

The rational administration of society is. . .detached from phenomena such as class conflict or group-specific interactions. . .purposive-rational action increasingly governs the institutions of society, the political framework of which is subverted by purposive-rational thinking that does not take into account the possibility of alternativeness either to the existing structure of domination or its policies. Technical rules replace societal norms as guidelines for political action, and rationalization is understood as a process which leads to "the growth of productive forces. . . the expansion of technical-administrative power" instead of "emancipation, individuation,. . .the expansion of domination-free communication.

What we have, then, is a social environment typified by technical knowledge and societal members believing that bureaucratic decisions are made with the rational pursuit of members' goals in mind. However, it is the rather large certainty that the social environment is controlled by bureaucratic interests in political manipulation that prompts us to keep a watchful eye on the social service bureaucracy as it interacts with the Hispanic community—especially during a time when an increasingly conservative environment is forcing major policy changes in the distribution of public goods to peripheral members (e.g., minority groups) in the society.

Finally, the exploratory and theoretical nature of our comments must be kept in mind. Should they encourage individuals, especially Hispanic scholars, to explore the varying parameters of the issue through empirical research, the primary mission of this essay will have been attained. Serious research attention—not just social science interest in reinforcing stereotypes concerning the institutional participation of Hispanics—must be directed to the political economy of social services for the Hispanic community. It may be that in studying the role of Anglo-American institutions, researchers may obtain empirical support for the general belief among Hispanics that those institutions are inhibitive and manipulative.

NOTES

[1] This essay has benefited immensely from my conversations with Ralph Guzman, Michael Olivas, Eduardo Hernandez-Chavez, and my students. Comments I received from the staff of the Latino Institute in Chicago clarified central concepts and enhanced the policy implications for social service delivery outlined in the essay. Any shortcomings, however, are my own responsibility.

[2] U.S. Department of Commerce, Bureau of the Census, "Persons of Spanish Origin in the United States: March 1979" (Advance Report), Series P-20, No. 347, issued October 1980.

³ Sources focusing on these characteristics are: U.S. Commission on Civil Rights, *Social Indicators of Equality for Minorities and Women* (Washington,D.C.: Commission on Civil Rights, 1978); H. Edward Ransford, *Race and Class in American Society: Black/Chicano/Anglo* (Cambridge, Mass. Schenkman Publishing Co., 1977); Leslie J. Silverman, "The Educational Advantage of Language-Minority Persons in the United States," (Washington, D.C.: National Center for Education Statistics, 1978); Dorothy Waggoner, "Place of Birth and Language Characteristics of Persons of Hispanic Origin in the United States," (Washington, D.C.: National Center for Education Statistics, 1978); Leo F. Estrada, "Language and Political Consciousness Among the Spanish-Speaking in the United States: A Demographic Study," pp. 13-22 in D. J. R. Bruckner, ed., *Politics and Language: Spanish and English in the United States* (The University of Chicago: Center for Policy Study, 1980); and G. H. Brown, N. L. Rosen, S. T. Hill, M. A. Olivas, *The Condition of Education for Hispanic Americans* (Washington, D.C.: National Center for Education Statistics, 1980).

⁴ Julian Nava's appointment as U.S. Ambassador to Mexico will certainly go far in drawing that country's interest closer to the plight of Hispanics in the U.S. and will reinforce the U.S.'s position that it does take Hispanics seriously.

⁵ Implicit is the assumption that language becomes a vehicle of control as the individual is exposed to institutions, such as the mass media and educational systems, which are subject to indirect and direct political control.

⁶ In this essay, we will be primarily referring to welfare programs but will be using the term "social service bureaucracy" to refer to the global aggregation of such services as welfare, health, education, etc.

⁷ F. F. Piven and R. Cloward, *Regulating the Poor: The Functions of Public Welfare* (New York: Pantheon, 1971), p. 61.

⁸ Richard Quinney, *Class, State, and Crime* (New York: Longman, 1977).

⁹ James O'Conner, *The Fiscal Crisis of the State* (New York: St. Martin's Press, 1973), p. 161.

¹⁰ Hans Gerth and C. Wright Mills, *Character and Social Structures: The Psychology of Social Institutions* (New York: Harcourt, Brace, and World, 1953).

¹¹ Larry Hirschhorn suggests that social services are rational to the extent that they are functional to capitalist development by regulating the growth, structure, and development of the working poor. ("The Political Economy of Social Service Rationalization: A Developmental View," *Contemporary Crises* 2:63-81, 1978).

¹² Individuals usually construct models of choice based on past experiences and particularistic views of present stimuli. As a result, most expressed choices are *routine* in that they invoke solutions used before. As a result, when involved in problem-solving, an individual will conduct a limited search for alternatives along familiar paths, selecting the first satisfactory one that comes along.

¹³ Richard Edwards, *Contested Terrain: The Transformation of the Workplace in the Twentieth Century* (New York: Basic Books, 1979), p. 20.

¹⁴ One can argue that bureaucratic control operates because individuals are not conscious of their activities as definitions of self as much as they are thinking of attaining a satisfactory solution to their situation. The former implies recognition of one's immediate behavioral dispositions, whereas the latter implies that one becomes *aware* but not *conscious* of behavioral dispositions once a choice is made.

[15] Edwards, *Contested Terrain,* p. 86.

[16] Ralph Guzman, "La Repatriacion Farzosa Como Solucion Concluyente al Problema de la Immigracion Ilegal: Una Perspectiva Historica," Foro *Internacional* (Enero—Marzo 1978).

[17] Rodolfo Acuna, *Occupied America: The Chicano's Struggle Toward Liberation* (San Francisco: Canfield Press, 1972), pp. 190-95.

[18] The inclusion of documented immigrants produced the impression that voluntary repatriation was occurring rather than forced deportation.

[19] Acuna, *Occupied America;* Abraham Hoffman, *Unwanted Mexican Americans in the Great Depression* (Tucson: University of Arizona Press, 1974); Carey McWilliams, *North from Mexico* (Philadelphia: J.B. Lippincott, 1949); Emory S. Bogardus, *The Mexican in the United States* (Los Angeles: University of Southern California Press, 1934).

[20] Hofman, *Unwanted Mexican Americans,* p. 86.

[21] Quoted in Leo Grebler, Joan Moore, Ralph Guzman, *The Mexican American People* (New York: Free Press, 1970), p. 525.

[22] Despite promises by social workers that once economic conditions improved repatriated Mexican families would be able to return to the U.S., their exit cards designated that they had been charity cases, which automatically excluded them from reentry.

[23] According to the latest figures from the National Association of Social Workers, 92% of regularly employed social workers are white, 5% are black, and the remaining 3% are comprised of American Indians, Asian Americans, and Hispanics. (See David A. Hardcastle and Arthur J. Katz, *Employment and Unemployment in Social Work: A Study of NASW Members* (Washington, D.C.: National Association of Social Workers, Inc., 1979).

[24] See the following for a brief historical view of the issues in the legal literature: Note, "El Derecho de Aviso: Due Process and Bilingual Notice," *Yale Law Journal* 83 (1973) 385-400; Charles P. Adams, "Citado a Comparecer: Language Barriers and Due Process—Is Mailed Notice in English Constitutionally Sufficient?," *California Law Review* 61 (1973): 1395-1420.

[25] Mendoza Report, *Access of Non or Limited English Speaking Persons of Hispanic Origin to the New York City Department of Social Services* (U.S. Department of Health, Education, and Welfare: Office of Civil Rights, September 1978).

[26] Reported by Mario Obledo and Carlos Alcala, "Discrimination Against the Spanish Language in Public Service: A Policy Alternative," pp. 155-62 in D. J. R. Bruckner, ed., *Politics and Language: Spanish and English in the United States* (The University of Chicago: Center for Policy Study, 1980).

[27] C. Wright Mills, *The Sociological Imagination* (New York: Gorve Press, 1959), pp. 179-81.

[28] Toussaint Hocevar, "Equilibria in Linguistic Minority Markets," *Kyklos* 28 (1975): 337-57.

[29] For an interesting analysis, see John J. Halcon, "The Political Economy of Bilingual Bicultural Education," pp. 136-50 in Raymond V. Padilla, ed., *Bilingual Education and Public Policy in the United States* (Eastern Michigan University: Bilingual Bicultural Education Program, 1979).

[30] Concerning the conflict between blacks and Hispanics, see the Spring 1980 issue of the civil rights quarterly, *Perspectives.*

[31] C. F. Jurgen Habermas, *Communication and the Evolution of Society* (Boston: Beacon Press, 1979).

[32] Claus Mueller, *The Politics of Communication: A Study in the Political Sociology of Language, Socialization, and Legitimation* (New York: Oxford University Press, 1973), pp. 109-10.

Political Pressures Affecting Natural Resource Development on Indian Reservations

Carl L. Tahkofper

There are many political pressures—national, state and tribal—which affect natural resource development on Indian reservations. Generally, those forces affecting natural resources are the same ones affecting the exercise of tribal government. The two are so inextricably intertwined that it is difficult to enter a discussion of one without drawing in the other. A seemingly simple undertaking in natural resource management, such as a tribe developing and operating its own coal mine on a reservation, is fraught with potential governmental issues between tribes and states. For example, a state might feel that its regulatory authority rather than a tribes's should govern the operation; or might feel that its taxation authority and not a tribe's should prevail.

To place these influences in their proper perspective, this essay will focus on those sources which place pressure on the exercise of tribal government and thus the development and management of natural resources. Within the federal government, practices of all three branches will be considered. State governments and those entities closely aligned with them, the press and non-Indian court systems, will also receive some perusal. Finally, within reservations, tribal government itself and pressures placed on it by its membership will be discussed.

However, it is in order that prior to any such review, some scrutiny of the importance of Indian natural resources in comparison to public resources should take place. The source of the following information is the *Report To The Federal Trade Commission On Mineral Leasing On Indian Lands* prepared by the Bureau of Competition to the Federal Trade Commission in October 1975. Although the report is over six years old, there would be little appreciable change in its statistics. It is unfortunate that it covers Indian and public lands only; information concerning practices on private lands is not provided.

There are 271 Indian reservations and communities in the United States, with land categorized as follows:

Tribal Land	40,772,934 acres
Allotted Land	10,244,481 "
Ceded Land	2,157,959 "
Total Indian Lands	53,175,374 "

Indian Lands as a Percent of Total U.S. Lands: 2.3%

Coal

In 1974 there were 11 coal leases on Indian lands, covering approximately 285,753 acres, for an average of 23,523 acres per lease. By contrast, on public lands there were 463 coal leases, with an average acreage of only 1,470 acres. 52 of the 463 public lands leases (11%) were producing as compared to 4 of the 11 Indian coal leases (36%).

Cumulative and fiscal year 1974 coal production from Indian, public, and total U.S. lands:

	Cumulative (1920-1974)	*FY 1974*
Indian Lands	66,112,000 tons	11,508,000 tons
Public Lands	311,405,000 "	20,178,000 "
Total U.S.	26,977,858,000 "	595,500,000 "
Producing Indian Lands as a Percent of Total Producing Public and Indian Lands	17.5%	36.9%

Oil and Gas

As of 1974 there were 13,583 oil and gas leases on Indian lands and 97,812 oil and gas leases on all public lands. Collectively, the Indian land leases covered 4,187,644 acres, while such leases on public lands covered 72,546,188 acres. There were 23,111 producing leases on public lands. Thus in 1974 approximately 23.4% of Indian land oil and gas leases were producing compared to only 9.4% of public land oil and gas leases.

Cumulative and 1974 oil production from Indian, public, and total U.S. lands:

	Cumulative (1920-1974)	FY 1974
Indian Lands	956,905,000 barrels	30,685,000 barrels
Public Lands	4,990,317,000 "	168,782,000 "
Producing Indian Lands as a Percent of Total Producing Public and Indian Lands	16.1%	15.4%

Cumulative and Fiscal year 1974 gas production from Indian and public lands:

	Cumulative (1920-1974)	FY 1974
Indian Lands	2,311,800,000 MCF	125,080,000 MCF
Public Lands	16,589,702,000 "	1,049,699,000 "
Producing Indian Lands as a Percent of Total Producing Public and Indian Lands	13.8%	3.7%

Uranium

As of 1974 there were 380 uranium leases on Indian lands, as compared with only 4 on leased public and acquired lands. While Indian land leases covered an area of approximately 254,380 acres, leases on public and acquired lands equalled 3,808 acres. While 3 of the 380 Indian land uranium leases were producing, none of the public and acquired land leases were producing.

Cumulative and fiscal year 1974 crude uranium ore production from Indian lands and public and acquired lands:

	Cumulative (1920-1974)	FY 1974
Indian Lands	18,418,984 tons	1,136,739 tons
Public and Acquired Lands	211,542 "	0 "
Producing Indian Lands as a Percent of Total Producing Public and Acquired Lands	8,688.2%	

In 1974 the Atomic Energy Commission estimated that 16% of all recoverable uranium reserves were located on Indian lands. Public and acquired land reserves represented 24% of the total. Thus Indian land reserves constitute about two-thirds of the reserves on public and acquired lands.

As one can readily see, the contribution of Indian lands to the United States economy is disproportionately higher than that contributed by public lands. The reasons for this disparity will be discussed later.

National Political Pressures

Congress

It is the tacit policy of Congress to avoid legislation which provides for the long-term existence of Indian tribes. Indian tribes as governmental entities, and Indian reservations within the geographic areas of state governments, appear to be viewed by non-Indians and their government as temporary. Even though the United States solemnly and formally agreed to recognize the rights of Indians to govern the little territory they still held in return for their ceding millions of acres of their land, those contractual agreements have generally been ignored when it has been in the interest of the federal government to do so. In addition to that period of time when treaties with Indian tribes were blatantly broken, there has also existed in Congress a subtle practice of enacting or not enacting legislation making it difficult for tribal governments to survive on their own.

Because of their quasi-sovereign status, Indian tribes have always believed that they had the authority to enact taxation legislation within reservations to provide for some support of their governing programs. Indeed, some tribes have enacted taxation legislation similar to the severance tax placed on resources by state governments. But for the most part, tribes are inhibited from taking such actions because of the threat of state governments to challenge them. Tribes have never had the legal resources to counter such maneuvers that are available to state governments.

The objections by state governments are usually based on an ignorance of the prerogatives of tribal governments, or simply a belief that Indian tribes should not have the right to exist within their own territories and should be challenged at every opportunity. Congress is well aware of the difficulties faced by Indian tribes in enacting taxation, but it simply ignores their problems. A simple joint resolution by Congress which would clearly enunciate the governmental prerogatives of Indian tribes would easily clarify these rights.

In formulating legislation to provide financial assistance to manage natural resources within states, Congress avoids giving equal assistance to Indian tribes. Without such federal assistance, many of the natural resource management programs being conducted by state governments would simply collapse. Yet Indian tribes, if they hope to manage their resources at all, are somehow expected to function with much less. Federal funds for air quality, fish and game preservation, recreation, surface mining, and reclamation and range management are some of the areas in which states are provided with federal assistance. The federal recreation program managed by state governments is open to Indian tribes; however, it requires a 50 percent matching share by local government. Because of this matching requirement, it is rare to see an Indian tribe take advantage of the program.

In addition to legislation specifically established to provide assistance to states from general tax revenues, Congress has enacted legislation to allow state and county governments to share in the income from public lands. The Mineral Leasing Act of 1920 and the Taylor Grazing Act return to state and local government a large portion of the income from public lands. Indian tribes are not allowed to share in these returns. In 1968 Wyoming's royalty return amounted to $68 million from the Mineral Leasing Act alone. Incidentally, the Taylor Grazing Act provides cheap grass for cattle grazing in the national forests, but since its inception this provision has been totally dominated by white ranchers, even though some Indian reservations are adjacent to national forests.

Whenever Congress does enact legislation covering Indian minerals, it does not assist tribes in developing and managing their own resources as it does state governments; rather, it provides for the easy access to those minerals by industry. Public lands are governed by the Mineral Leasing Act of 1938. The 1920 act is fairly strict in its provisions; however, it does provide for a royalty return to the federal government on oil and gas, for example, at a rate between 12½% and 25%, depending on the amount of production. The 1938 Act, which governs Indian land leasing, has been described as "flexible." It provides for a flat 16⅔% royalty for oil and gas, and unlike the 1920 Act limiting leases to 2,560 acres, allows for leases of much greater acreage. In the foregoing section it may be noted that the average size coal lease on Indian lands was 23,523 acres, while leases on public lands averaged 1,470 acres.

In reading of such machinations by Congress, one might be inclined to ask just who represents Indian people in the national legislature. Indians ask the same questions. In many instances, their own state delegation is hostile and works against tribes rather than for them. Indians sometimes joke that they need the Eastern liberals to save them from their own congressmen and senators. In some cases, this is not an exaggeration. The political impotence of Indian people makes it necessary that occasionally a Kennedy or an Abourezk step forward to represent them.

Federal Administration

The policy of the federal administration aligns itself closely with that of Congress. It treats Indian lands as public lands, and the return from public lands of the United States is as low as anyplace in the world. It provides very little management and governmental support to tribes. Although it could provide financial assistance to them, without any cost to the federal government, it refuses to do so. In its role as trustee of Indian lands, it shows less than enthusiastic support in its litigative efforts to protect the rights of Indian people and tribes.

The federal government has always treated public lands as if they were the private domain of industry. This attitude seems to have originated during that period of immigrant history when railroad companies were given every other section of land for forty miles on either side of constructed railroads. For a pittance these companies received millions of acres, mineral rights included. The giveaway price that is charged for public lands and minerals establishes the price for lands around it, including Indian lands. Tribes may feel that their minerals are worth much more, but industry merely needs to point to the price for public lands and responds that it would be foolish to pay more for Indian minerals.

The reflection of this giveaway policy is perhaps best exemplified in the mineral leases covering Indian lands themselves. The acreage limitation on Indian lands, 2,560 acres—the same as on public lands—is waived with very little justification. It is in fact rare to discover a lease that complies with the acreage limitation. In addition, the lessee may be given free use of the surface for processing facilities, free water for processing or generating facilities, and free transmission line easements. One consultant who has assisted in negotiating leases throughout the free world, quite often for countries which have recently freed themselves from colonial status, terms the leases for U.S. Indian minerals the most archaic in the world.

As it does for states, the federal government could easily assist tribes in the management of resources. However, it does not. It would appear such assistance might violate the intent of contributing nothing that would lead to a permanent tribal government. The management of tribal forests and grasslands is given some attention, but other areas of natural resources are totally ignored. Fish and wildlife management, mineral inventories, development and management, and protection of air quality are a few of the little-considered resource areas.

In 1975 the Secretary of the Interior placed a moratorium on the approval of any tribal water management codes. The codes establish regulations under which water resources within reservations could be used and managed. In most tribal constitutions established under the authority of the Indian Reorganization Act of 1934, the Secretary is given arbitrary approval responsibility over many tribal actions, water codes included. The reasoning of the Secretary in 1975 was that Indian water rights were in such a state of fluctuation that tribes should wait until the courts provided some degree of certainty.

Since 1975, however, state governments have enacted and implemented a wealth of water legislation which they are attempting to impose upon the vacuum of regulations found on Indian reservations. The damage being generated by the Secretarial moratorium is incalculable at this time.

The federal government's lack of assistance in providing exploration assistance is particularly glaring. Leases over both public and Indian lands do not require that any exploration data be made available to the U.S. Geological Survey or to Indian tribes. As a result, tribes have no idea of the mineral development potential on their lands. Since the U.S. Geological Survey does some exploration work on public lands, more is known of the mineral potential there. Despite numerous requests, however, the U.S. Geological Survey has resisted doing for tribes the same services that it provides for public lands. Reasons given for this resistance are that it does not have the personnel for that undertaking and questions whether or not it has such a mandate in the first place. It is interesting to note that the Office of General Counsel of the Department Of Energy is also examining that same issue. Does D.O.E. have a mandate to provide exploration assistance to tribes?

Although there is a proportionately greater amount of Indian acreage under lease for minerals as well as production than on public lands, the competition within industry for public land minerals is much greater. On Indian lands a tract up for lease may get one or two bids, or in many cases none at all, usually depending on whether a company or the Bureau of Indian Affairs nominated it for advertising in the first place. Meanwhile, on public lands a tract may have ten, twelve, or more bidders. The greater the competition, of course, the higher the bonus return. The reason for this disparity in competition between Indian and public lands is the fact that the exploration information generated by the U.S. Geological Survey over public lands is made available to industry prior to any advertisement. Obviously, much more interest is shown when some exploration data are available. Because there is not similar information available concerning Indian lands, interest and competition are considerably less.

As mentioned previously, direct financial asistance to tribes could be provided without any cost to the federal government. These funds could provide for the management of natural resources. Several years ago, on its own initiative, the federal government entered into water marketing agreements with state governments whereby several hundred thousand acre feet of water behind federally constructed dams on the Missouri River were given gratis to state governments. States sell this water to any and all users and deposit the proceeds into their general funds. The states are not required to construct any transportation facilities which remain the total responsibility of the user.

When Indian tribes became aware of these water marketing agreements, they felt they should also have the opportunity to participate. Many of the dams and reservoirs were constructed on Indian reservations, resulting in not only a great loss of land but also causing additional jurisdictional problems between tribes, states, and numerous federal agencies over who was to now regulate hunting and fishing, water use, recreation, and development. Considering the particular impositions placed on tribes to construct the dams and reservoirs, one would think it appropriate that the federal government would have first approached Indian tribes with the water marketing concept. Not only has the federal government not done this, but it has thus far resisted every attempt to allow Indian tribes to participate.

There is yet another source of funding that should be made available to tribes, but because of disinterest shown by the federal government is not. The Public Works Act of 1965, the basic legislation under which the Department of Commerce operates, created among other things regional planning commissions. The Four Corners Commission and the Old West Regional Commission operate in the Rocky Mountain area. One portion of the mandate given the regional planning commissions is to provide planning assistance for the impacts of energy development within their regions. The commissions, which each has a budget of $7 to 8 million a year, have provided minimal assistance to tribes. For example, in the eight years of its existence, the Old West Regional Commission has granted funds to one Montana tribe, one South Dakota tribe, and a Colorado urban Indian organization. The total of its grants to tribes amounts to less than one-half million dollars. The governors of the eight states within the Old West Commission form the board of directors, and in reality the $7 to 8 million becomes a slush fund for the governors. The funds are distributed to state organizations and non-state organizations which become the favorites of the governors and their respective research efforts. Indian tribes have thus far been unable to participate as equal partners with the federal and state governments in the preparation of regional and site specific impact statements. Given the regional planning mandate, one would think that tribes should be able to participate along with states in the use of these funds, and yet they do not. There is on each regional planning commission a federal co-chairman whose function is to assist in guiding and monitoring the work of the commissions. In reality, one never hears a peep out of the co-chairman, and the political abuses of the commissions continue unabated.

In its role as trustee of Indian lands, Indians, and tribes, the federal government shows very little enthusiasm as a protector of Indian rights. Many of the enabling acts under which territories achieved statehood required that states enact constitutions with so-called disclaimer clauses. These clauses proclaimed that states would leave Indian tribes to govern themselves and not attempt to impose state jurisdiction over them. Despite such language in the enabling acts and state constitutions, states have ignored congressional intent and have tried and continue to employ any means to swallow Indian reservations and limit tribal government. It seems that states are encouraged since their blatant disregard of the enabling acts has drawn no slap of their hands by the federal government. The Solicitor's Offices within both the Department of the Interior and the Department of Justice, which are charged with initiating and conducting litigation on behalf of Indians and tribes, are slow to act against state encroachment. Even when persuaded to take action on behalf of tribes, it cannot always be counted on to construct a vigorous defense. In many cases it is willing to concede to the opposition without putting up a fight. In one water rights case in the State of Washington, it was in such opposition to the tribe and its personal attorneys that the tribe formally petitioned the court to have the United States declared a hostile witness.

Several tribes and an intertribal organization in the Northwestern United States have been attempting for years to establish an annual meeting with the Justice Department to discuss and plan future litigation on behalf of tribes. The Justice Department has steadfastly refused such a meeting and continues to arbitrarily pick and choose litigation which it feels is appropriate.

Supreme Court

Early in American history, when Indian tribes were being destroyed and obliterated as fast as the federal government could find the strength, a phenomenon totally contrary to the practices of that period occurred. Chief Justice John Marshall and his court, through a series of decisions, began to make it difficult for the federal government and states to legally decimate Indian tribes. These decisions took away the authority of state governments to deal with tribes, investing it in the federal government. Tribes were declared to be quasi-sovereign, possessing many powers of self-government. These decisions, showing some compassion for a people being force-marched out of their homeland east of the Mississippi, led President Andrew Jackson to remark that since John Marshall was making the decisions, the justice could also enforce them. In reality, however, the decisions did little to slow the removal and extermination of the Indian people, which continued for another fifty or sixty years. What was important was that the Supreme Court decisions remained as law, for the most part undisturbed. After Indian tribes were placed on reservations and the United States made a concerted effort to obliterate the leadership of tribes and extricate Indians from what remaining land they had, a gradual change of policy took place. Finally in 1934 the Indian Reorganization Act, which recognized the right of tribal self-government, provided the forum by which tribes could establish their own form of government.

The breaking up of tribal lands into individual allotments ceased. The Homestead laws, which allowed non-Indians to settle on Indian reservations, were discontinued. As tribes established their constitutions, the inherent self-governing powers and Supreme Court decisions that had been lying dormant for so long were gradually incorporated into tribal government. State, county and local governments, which had been riding roughshod over Indian reservations for scores of years—assuming control over what they felt like assuming—were treating tribal governments as if they were a farce. However, as tribes became more experienced in governmental affairs, they began to question the presence of non-Indian governments within their reservations and to remove them where there existed blatant disregard of tribal rights. Soon tribes and non-Indians were litigating one jurisdictional issue after another, primarily in federal courts. Since the Supreme Court had only the Marshall Court decisions to rely on, many cases were settled in favor of tribes. Jurisdictional issues relating to natural resources, water, coal, fish and wildlife, facilities siting, zoning, and taxation are currently awaiting court decision. In one of its more recent findings, which many feel is nothing more than outright racism, the Supreme Court of the United States declared that Indian tribes did not have the right to arrest and try non-Indians for violations of tribal law.

State Political Pressures

State Government

In the minds of Native Americans, one of the most puzzling phenonmenon of this immigrant nation is the psychological make-up of white people. What is it that drives them to covet everything the native people of this country possess? Native Americans reason that after the millions and millions of acres they have given up, and after having been reduced to poverty and living on small fractions of their former lands, the whites would be content to leave them alone. But no; they are like the old buffalo hunter who after slaughtering all the buffalo for tongues and hides now returns to pick up the bones. Whites themselves point out the disgracefulness and unchristian behavior of their history in dealing with native peoples. But like an alcoholic with little control over his mind, they return to continue the consumption. It is like a sickness among white people.

This sickness is manifested most clearly in state governments and their political entities which have within their geographical boundaries one or more Indian reservations and a large Indian population. The degree to which each state attacks tribal governments varies, but generally their activities are similar. In one state an annual meeting is held composed of the governor and his department chiefs and aides. The agenda is totally devoted to the plan of attack against Indian rights for the coming year in the form of state-initiated litigation, state legislation, and legislation for which it will lobby in the national legislature. The lobbying efforts also continue within organizations in which state and local employees participate, such as Western governors' organizations, national state attorney generals' organizations, national county commissioners' organizations, etc.

Generally, each state maintains a set of special statistics—propaganda, if you will—covering Indian-related problems such as how much money the state is losing in taxation to Indians, crime statistics, and other negative social data. Tribes have asked that state governments also maintain data that indicate how states are particularly benefiting from reservations, or what little amount of state tax funds are actually spent thereon, but to no avail.

States generally maintain a research effort, usually funded through the regional planning commissions, which feeds information to litigative and legislative actions directed against tribes. Indians have of course been unsuccessful at obtaining the results of this research.

As previously stated, Indian tribes have found that their participation in federal programs is minimal as administered by state governments. Again in the area of natural resource management, many states have legislatively established commissions to negotiate a range of disagreements with tribes. Because these commissions have sat at the negotiating table with the attitude that "What's mine is mine, and what's your is negotiable," it is a rarity to find even minor agreement between states and tribes.

Many states have enacted severance tax legislation, which among other things is partially used to assist local governments in offsetting the impacts of energy development. In Montana, a state with a 30% severance on coal—a large portion of which comes from Indian lands—the state attorney general has declared that Indian tribes are not eligible to receive coal impact funds. The opinion is a racist one, but it is not uncommon. Because states have blocked the use of any tax funds originating from Indian minerals as means of alleviating the impacts of energy development, tribes have pushed for national legislation. However, Western governors are now proposing to Congress that any future federal impact funds be distributed through the states.

State Press Coverage

A large portion of the press coverage in those states where Indian reservations are located is tilted toward the objectives of state government. Statements and issues as described by state government are repeated in the editorial pages. Seldom if ever does one see editorials examining the reasoned position of Indian tribes and people.

In one instance in the Northern plains, the Federal Bureau of Investigation was feeding inflamatory statements to the press about forthcoming hostile actions of the American Indian Movement. Without verifying the truth of the reports, several newspapers simply printed what they were told. The news caused consternation and fear among both Indians and non-Indians, causing many to cancel their annual participation in local social events. Needless to say, when the hostile actions did not occur as forecast, there was no self-examination among the press about printing at face value what they had been fed by the FBI. A large portion of the coverage of Indian/state jurisdictional disputes publicizes the resulting disorder. There is always a following implication that in the interest of "good government" the dispute ought to resolved in favor of the state.

On or near many reservations there appears to be an effort to exaggerate any disorder that is found on them. If an Indian judge is charged with driving while intoxicated, the press coverage is unusually extensive. If a non-Indian county judge is charged with driving while intoxicated, the incident is given no or minor press coverage. Crime, negative social conditions, any misappropriation of funds among Indian people or tribes, gets ballyhooed out of all proportion by the press.

On the other hand, if Indians or tribes take some action that benefits both the reservation and the non-Indian community, the action is reported without comment. The Northern Cheyenne tribe was the first entity in the United States to invoke the provisions of the Clean Air Act and change the air quality over their reservation to a Class 1 status. This status means that industry will not be able to pollute the Northern Cheyenne reservation to the same degree that it does the surrounding areas in the huge coal fields of Southeastern Montana. Good air quality obviously benefits non-Indians near the reservation as well, but the state press found itself unable to give a single word of praise to the Northern Cheyennes—while one widely circulated environmentalist paper named the tribe "Environmentalists of the Year." Much publicity is also given to any grant of federal funds provided to tribes. The headlines seem to shout, "Look at our tax money being thrown out to these non-taxpaying Indians"

State and Federal District Courts

Studying the Indian Reorganization Act, that legislation mentioned earlier which provided for the form of tribal government, one notes that the original version of the bill provided for a court system which would handle all matters of substance originating on Indian reservations; its levels of appeal were to be the circuit courts of appeal and ultimately the Supreme Court of the United States. Unfortunately for Indians, the final bill eliminated the court system provision. Under other authority Indian courts were established, but with limited powers in comparison to what was originally contemplated.

For nearly all matters of substance, Indians have been forced into an immigrant peoples' court system. In the majority of cases, the courts have been hostile and the racism in the decisions hard to hide. State courts have been particularly hostile, and for the most part Indians have been able to avoid them. But within the last several years Congress and the Supreme Court have been giving greater and greater jurisdiction over natural resource matters to state courts. Increasingly, more water rights litigation contesting jurisdiction between states and tribes is being settled in state courts. Indians feel that their chances of obtaining justice in such forums are purely accidental.

Although federal district courts are not part of the state system nor organizationally controlled by state government, they are mentioned here because the judges presiding over them are in fact state politicians. Federal judges are usually chosen from defrocked politicians and defeated senators and congressmen. It is rare to find a senator or congressman who, in moving up the political ladder, has not also served in his or her state legislature. Yet somehow a former state legislator and advocate of state jurisdiction above Indian jurisdiction is, by congressional action, supposed to dismiss prejudices and become an unbiased judge. Although Indian tribes have found federal district courts less prejudicial than state courts, they would still like to see the first Indian judge. Indians have protested to the Senate Judiciary Committee and requested participation in the selection process for both federal judges and district attorneys, but have thus far received noncommittal replies.

Tribal Pressures Affecting Natural Resource Development

Governmental Structure

The governmental form on most reservations is simply inadequate to the task of a modern administration. All power is situated in a single body—the council. There is no formally established structure beneath the council to carry on day-to-day and year-to-year work. The infrastructure to handle the powers of government as well as the management of natural resources simply does not exist on the majority of reservations.

As a result, there is no continuity of action from one election to the next. Action that one council implemented for very good reasons may be reversed by the following council for very good reasons. The lack of delegated and delineated powers, as well as laws that are easily changed, results in a forum for arbitrary rule. The structure does not even make the council answerable to those who elected it, and some councils even go so far as to not record individual votes.

It would obviously be difficult to establish a solid and dependable infrastructure for natural resource management under such a forum. And as would be expected, the mineral deals that Indian tribes make reflect this inadequacy. In addition, tribes find it difficult to request and hire the kinds of people who could assist them.

Tribes often begin to see the need for an infrastructure when some of the mineral agreements proposed to them call for an influx of a large amount of non-Indian people to work under the contract. They learn that controls for zoning, housing, sanitation, water use, facility siting, and many other relevant problem areas, have not been established and implemented. Tribes also become aware that when state governments see any such vacuum, they quickly try to fill it with their own laws and regulations.

Another fact that inhibits councils from making mineral agreements is that, for the most part, the tax infrastructure needed to take advantage of mineral agreements on reservations does not exist. Industry and states have always benefited from these agreements to an extraordinarily higher degree than have Indian tribes. If tribes come to mineral agreements without tax structures in place, they know state governments will quickly impose their own.

In many cases, councils simply lack the integrity to oppose bad mineral agreements. Pressure from industry and their own people for tribal dividend payments caves in any resistance. In such cases, they hope that the Bureau of Indian Affairs will save them from their own imprudence and disapprove the agreements.

Tribal Membership

There has been created among Indian people a strong sense of dependency, a feeling that it is not necessary to work in order to live. Uncle Sam or the tribe will come through with a handout when the going gets difficult. The reasons for this dependency are many: the taking away of the land and thus much of the means by which Indian people made their living; the policy on the part of the federal government to refrain from encouraging or assisting tribes in managing their own affairs; the "We can do it better for you" approach; and the sheer practice of giving people something for nothing.

As a consequence, large portions of the Indian population living on reservations have not had the opportunity to learn how to work. They have learned how to survive without it. A further consequence of receiving something for nothing is that what is received is held in low esteem and often treated with outright disrespect. This portion of a reservation population brings a lot of pressure on councils for charity funds and tribal dividend payments, and pays little heed to what must be given up to obtain such funds.

Pressure is also applied to tribal councils for mineral agreements and subsequent tribal dividends from another quarter—tribal members who live off-reservation, generally at a considerable distance, and who do not intend to return to the reservation to derive any benefit from it except that which they receive through tribal dividend payments. They are not much interested in hearing of possible physical harm that might come to the reservation, nor of consequences to people there as a result of the agreements. This is the same group who push the hardest for termination of the reservation, that is, selling all assets and distributing the return to tribal members.

As related above, there are a variety of pressures affecting the management and development of Indian natural resources. Much of what was reported is clearly negative. But despite all the obstacles, Indian tribes have an opportunity as never before in their history to make their valuable natural resources work for them. A few tribes leading the way can turn past practices of reservation development completely around. The income from natural resource agreements made prudently or developed by Indians on their own can support the effort needed in the exercise of genuine tribal government. Indian leadership nurtured since the Indian Reorganization Act is emerging in the numbers needed to make necessary changes. A greater awareness of the workings of industry and business is gradually becoming apparent in the day-to-day administration of tribal government. The opportunity to properly support Indian tribes is at hand.

Racial and Educational Composition of the All-Volunteer Army

Charles C. Moskos, Jr.

Northwestern University

Since 1973 the United States has sought to accomplish what it has never attempted before—to maintain two million persons on active military duty on a completely voluntary basis. Debate on the all-volunteer force has come to include questions of the representativeness of those joining the forces as well as whether the quantity of recruits is sufficient. The rising proportion of black entrants, especially in the Army's enlisted ranks, has generated more heat than any other topic in the debate on the all-volunteer force. It is my contention, however, that the rising minority content in the Army actually masks a more pervasive and cross-racial shift in the social class bases of the lower enlisted ranks.

The plan of this study is straightforward. First, data are presented on the racial and educational background of the all-volunteer force, with a focus on the Army's enlisted ranks and the combat arms. Second, there is a discussion of the issue of representativeness and how this relates to soldierly performance and definitions of military service. Finally, policy considerations are raised which link serving in the ranks of the all-volunteer force with broader issues of citizen participation and national service.

Black Participation

In the quarter-century following World War II, black participation in the American military grew gradually. It has only been since the mid-1970s, as shown in table 1, that black membership in the armed forces exceeded the approximate 12 percent of blacks within the general population. It is to be stressed that the various services differ in their racial composition. The pattern has been for the Army to have the highest proportion of blacks, followed in order by the Marine Corps, Air Force, and Navy. Thus in 1979 blacks accounted for 28.9 percent of the Army, 19.8 percent of the Marine Corps, 13.8 percent of the Air Force, and 9.7 percent of the Navy. These percentages include both officer and enlisted personnel.

TABLE 1

BLACKS IN THE ARMED FORCES AS A PERCENTAGE OF TOTAL PERSONNEL
BY SELECTED YEARS

Year	Total Armed Forces	Army	Navy	Air Force	Marine Corps
1945	7.3	9.8	5.0	4.0[a]	3.6
1954	7.9	11.3	3.2	7.5	5.9
1965	9.5	12.8	5.2	9.2	8.3
1970	9.8	12.1	4.8	10.0	10.2
1975	14.3	19.9	7.2	12.5	16.7
1979	19.0	28.9	9.7	13.8	19.8

Source: Department of Defense statistics.
[a]1945 Air Force Figures refer to Army Air Corps.

Because the issue of racial content has been most pronounced in the all-volunteer Army, the largest of the services, our attention will primarily be on the Army. As given in table 2, black content varies by pay grade, although the overriding trend has been toward greater black participation at all levels. Blacks made up 11.8 percent of enlisted personnel in 1964, the last peacetime year before the war in Vietnam; 17.5 percent in 1972, the last year of the draft; and 32.2 percent in 1979. At senior noncom levels (E7-E9), blacks are considerably better represented in 1979 than at any earlier time. This reflects the black reenlistment rate in the 1970s being 1.7 times greater than that of whites. At the noncom level, we can expect blacks to play an increasingly important and stabilizing role. Blacks continue to be underrepresented in the officer corps, with the partial exception of company grade officers. A disproportionately white officer corps coupled with a disproportionately black enlisted component will be one of the key sociological considerations in the Army leadership of the 1980s.

TABLE 2
PERCENTAGE OF BLACK PARTICIPATION IN THE ARMY BY PAY GRADE

	1964	1972	1979
Officers:			
0-7 and above (general)	—	1.8	5.2
0-6 (colonel)	.2	1.5	4.3
0-5 (lieutenant colonel)	1.1	5.3	5.3
0-4 (major)	3.5	5.0	4.5
0-3 (captain)	5.1	3.9	6.9
0-2 (1st lieutenant)	3.6	3.4	9.7
0-1 (2nd lieutenant)	2.6	2.2	9.4
Warrant	2.8	4.5	5.9
Total Officers	3.3	3.9	6.8
Enlisted:			
E-9 (Sergeant major)	3.3	8.6	19.0
E-8 (master sergeant)	5.8	14.4	23.9
E-7 (sergeant first class)	7.9	19.9	25.2
E-6 (staff sergeant)	12.2	23.9	22.8
E-5 (sergeant)	14.8	16.9	28.6
E-4 (specialist 4)	12.5	14.1	33.7
E-3 (private first class)	11.9	16.7	37.8
E-2 (private)	11.6	18.5	37.9
E-1 (private)	6.4	18.4	37.3
Total Enlisted	11.8	17.4	32.2

Source: Department of Army statistics.

It is important to note that the trend toward increasing black content in the Army predates the all-volunteer force. The rising percentage of blacks has occurred somewhat independently of the end of conscription and can be attributed in part to the dramatic increase in the number of blacks eligible for military service. Most notable are the number of black high school graduates and the percentage of blacks placing in the upper levels of the mental aptitude tests required for service entry.[1] There is also the combined push of the astoundingly high unemployment rate among black youth and the pull of an institution which has perhaps gone further than any other to attack racism.

Since the advent of the all-volunteer Army, the proportion of black entrants has almost tripled over pre-Vietnam levels. As shown in table 3, black enlistees reached 36 percent of non-prior-service males in 1979 and 40 percent of females. Although the number of other minorities is not as reliably tabulated, increasing numbers of Hispanics have also been joining the all-volunteer Army. That well over 40 percent of

those entering the Army in the late 1970s were from minority groups
would be a reasonable estimate.

TABLE 3
BLACK PROPORTION OF ARMY ENLISTEES, MALE AND FEMALE
(Non-Prior-Service)

| | Percentage Black | |
Fiscal Year	Male	Female
1973	20.9	18.9
1974	27.9	19.1
1975	23.3	19.3
1976	24.9	18.2
1977	30.1	21.5
1978	34.9	30.3
1979	36.2	40.8

Source: Army Recruiting Command statistics.

Within the Army's enlisted ranks, racial content varies by branch
(the following figures are drawn from 1979 statistical data). Black
membership in the infantry is 30.6 percent. Thus it cannot be stated
that blacks are overrepresented in the combat arms in terms of total
enlisted blacks. Of course, blacks are overly proportionate in the infantry in relation to their numbers in American society, but this is because whites are underrepresented in the all-volunteer Army. Within
the Army, it is in support units where racial imbalance is most clearly
evident. Blacks tend to be concentrated in low-skill fields: 57.1 percent in petroleum handling; 46.8 percent in supply; and 45.1 percent in
wire maintenance. Whites, on the other hand, are disproportionately
represented in such high-skill fields as intercept equipment, signal intelligence, aviation, and electronics.

Race and Education

It is a well-recognized fact that the educational levels of blacks in
America have trailed behind that of whites. The trend, however, has
been toward a narrowing of the gap. Looking at males age 18-19 years
in 1967, for example, one notes that 30.7 percent of blacks compared to
15.4 percent of whites had not completed high school. By 1977 the high
school dropout rate for blacks had declined to 23.8 percent, while the
white rate increased to 17.0.[2] Still, even for the more recent period,
black educational attainment does fall behind that of whites.

Yet contrary to national patterns, the intersect of race and education is quite different among male entrants in the all-volunteer Army. Since the end of the draft, the proportion of black high school graduates entering the Army has exceeded that of whites, and this trend is becoming more pronounced. In 1979, as shown in table 4, high school graduates accounted for 65 percent of entering blacks compared to 54 percent of entering whites. In point of fact, today's Army enlisted ranks is the only major arena in American society where black educational levels surpass that of whites, and by a significant margin.

TABLE 4
PERCENTAGE OF HIGH SCHOOL GRADUATES AMONG ARMY MALE ENLISTEES BY RACE
(Non-Prior-Service)

Fiscal Year	Black	White
1975	59	53
1976	63	53
1977	65	53
1978	76	65
1979	65	54

Source: Army Recruiting Command statistics.

What may be happening in the all-volunteer Army, I suggest, is something like the following. Whereas the black soldier is fairly representative of the black community in terms of education and social background, white entrants of recent years are coming from the least-educated sectors of the white community. My visits with Army line units also leave the distinct impression that many of our young enlisted white soldiers are coming from non-metropolitan areas. I am even more impressed by what I do not often find in line units—urban and suburban white soldiers of middle-class background. In other words, the all-volunteer Army is attracting not only a disproportionate number of minorities, but also an unrepresentative segment of white youth who are, if anything, even more uncharacteristic of the broader social mix than are our minority soldiers.

It is startling to learn that among first-term soldiers in all the combat arms—infantry, artillery, armor, combat engineers—there were only 25 college graduates (out of 100,860 men) in 1980.

Recruitment into the Combat Arms

Following World War II there was a major shift within the military system toward greater technical complexity and greater reliance on support services. This corresponded with a decline in the proportion of men assigned to the combat arms. Since the early 1960s, however, there has been relative stability in the task distribution of soldiers. Presented in table 5, along with concomitant black-white distributions, are figures comparing the percentage of Army enlisted personnel in the combat arms for the years 1945, 1962, 1970, and 1980. Whereas in 1962 and 1970 blacks were twice as likely to be assigned to the combat arms than their proportion in the total Army, by 1980 blacks were slightly less likely than whites to be assigned to combat roles. It is to be repeated, however, that blacks in 1980 were still disproportionately represented in the combat arms in terms of their numbers in American society, if not in the context of their proportion in the Army.

TABLE 5

WHITE AND BLACK ARMY ENLISTED PERSONNEL IN THE COMBAT ARMS BY SELECTED YEARS

Category	1945[a]	1962	1970	1980
Percentage of total personnel in combat arms	44.5	26.0	23.8	26.4
Percentage of total white personnel in combat arms	48.2	24.9	23.4	26.6
Percentage of total black personnel in combat arms	12.1	33.4	26.0	25.1
Blacks as percentage of total personnel	10.5	12.2	13.5	32.6

Source: Department of Army statistics.
[a] Excludes Army Air Corps.

Another vantage on the social composition of the combat arms in 1980 can be gained from the data presented in tables 6 and 7. Table 6 simply reports the educational and racial background of the combat arms compared to the non-combat arms. Table 7 shows the likelihood of a soldier being assigned to the combat arms in terms of educational and racial background. The likelihood of a combat arms assignment is greater for high school dropouts (36.0 percent) than for high school graduates (26.9 percent). This is not a particularly surprising finding. But it is less of an expectation to find that white soldiers are more likely to be assigned to the combat arms than are black soldiers of similar educational level.

TABLE 6
MILITARY ASSIGNMENTS OF ARMY PERSONNEL BY EDUCATION AND RACE, 1980
(First-Termers)

Educational Level and Race	Combat Arms		Non-Combat Arms	
Non-High School Graduate	40.0%		30.1%	
White		26.8		19.0
Black		10.8		9.3
Other		2.4		1.8
High School Graduate	60.0		69.9	
White		34.3		39.3
Black		21.4		27.4
Other		4.3		3.2
Total	100.0%		100.0%	

Source: recomputed from Department of Army statistics.

TABLE 7
ARMY ENLISTED PERSONNEL IN COMBAT ARMS BY EDUCATION AND RACE, 1980
(First-Termers)

Percentage of Army Non-High School Graduates	
Who Are in Combat Arms	36.0
White	37.4
Black	33.0
Percentage of Army High School Graduates	
Who are in Combat Arms	26.9
White	27.1
Black	24.9

Source: recomputed from Department of Army statistics.

There can be no question that since the end of the draft, the Army has undergone a metamorphosis in its enlisted membership. It is, however, another kind of question as to whether this is good, bad, or irrelevant.

The clearest evidence bearing upon the effects of social background on soldierly performance deals with enlisted attrition. Since the end of the draft, about one in three service members does not complete his or her initial term of enlistment. Put another way, since 1973 over 600,000 young people have been prematurely discharged from the military for reasons of indiscipline, personality disorders, job inaptitude, and the like. The striking finding is that high school graduates are twice more likely than high school dropouts to complete their enlistments. More revealing, this finding is virtually unchanged when mental aptitude is held constant. High school graduates from the lower aptitude levels are actually much more likely to finish their tours than high school dropouts in the higher aptitude levels. Data which show black-white breakdowns indicate that overall attrition rates between the races are comparable, with the main exception being that blacks in the lower aptitude levels do better than their white counterparts.[3]

Other measures of soldierly performance, such as enlisted productivity and low disciplinary actions, show precisely the same correlates as found for attrition rates. High school graduates significantly outperform high school dropouts in the aggregate. Possession of a high school diploma, it seems, reflects the acquisition of social traits (work habits, punctuality, *Sitzfleisch*) which make for a more successful military experience. Despite the overwhelming evidence that the higher the educational quality, the better the soldierly performance, it is too frequently argued that there are many manual tasks for which bright soldiers are less adept than the not-so-bright. One Congressman has seriously proposed that the services purposively recruit more heavily from the less intelligent in order to fill menial jobs.[4] This assertion has the apparent attraction of making a virute out of a perceived necessity. But the facts are unambiguous—higher educated soldiers do better in low-skill jobs as well as in high-skill jobs.[5]

The military has always recruited large numbers of youth, white and black, who had no real alternative job prospects. Moreover, the military will continue to draw disproportionately from young blacks as long as they are victims of certain structural defects in the national economy—specifically, the steady flow of manufacturing jobs away from cities where so many poor blacks are trapped. But present trends toward labeling the Army as a recourse for America's underclasses are damaging for the youth involved precisely because they directly counter the premise that military participation is one of broadly-based national service. From the 1940s through the mid-1960s, the military served as a bridging environment between entering low-status youth and eventual middle-class employment.[6] Whatever successes the military had as a remedial organization for deprived youth were largely due to the armed forces being legitimated on other than overt welfare grounds—e.g., national defense, citizenship obligation, even manly honor.[7] In other words, those very conditions peculiar to the armed forces which serve to resocialize poverty youth toward productive ends depend directly upon the military not being defined as a welfare agency or as an employer of last resort. It will be increasingly difficult for the Army to avoid the characterization as a recourse for dead-end youth, even if unfair, unless enlisted membership reflects a cross-section of American youth.

To what degree the changing racial composition of the Army reflects white reluctance to join an increasingly black organization is unknown, though it is surely a factor. Yet I am unpersuaded that any significant number of middle-class whites—or middle-class of any race, for that matter—would be more likely to join the Army under present recruitment incentives, even if the Army were overwhelmingly white. That the disproportionately white Navy and the racially-balanced Air Force also have recruitment problems indicate that there is more than racial content at work in attracting a cross-section of youth to serve in the all-volunteer military.

The distinctive quality of the enlisted experience starting with World War II was the mixing of social classes and, beginning with the Korean War, the integration of races. This gave deprived youth an opportunity to test themselves, often successfully, against more privileged youth. Such enforced leveling of persons from different social backgrounds had no parallel in any other existing institution in American society; it was an elemental fact underlying enlisted service. This state of affairs began to diminish during the Vietnam War when the college-educated avoided service, and it has all but disappeared in the all-volunteer Army. These observations are to be placed in the context of recent studies which show all-volunteer soldiers displaying levels of alienation far exceeding that of the contemporary youth population or of World War II soldiers.[8]

From a historical standpoint, the evidence is also clear that military participation and combat risks in World War II were more equally shared by American men than in either the Korean or Vietnam wars. The draft *per se* is thus no guarantee that military participation will insure class equity. In the event of future hostilities, it is naive if not duplicitous to state that disproportionately high black casualties will have no or only minor consequences on the domestic political scene. It is important to remember the controversies which surrounded black casualty rates during the Vietnam War—this despite the fact, as will be reported in table 8, that black casualties in total were not disproportionate to the black percentage of the American population. Studies of Vietnam War casualties have documented that low social class (not race *per se*) was the grouping most strongly correlated with high casualties suffered by Americans in that war.[9] In light of the Vietnam experience, we can expect outrage—and properly so—if minority casualties were to range between 30 and 50 percent of the total. In these circumstances, the effectiveness of the U.S. Army could be irremediably undermined.

TABLE 8
BLACKS AS A PERCENTAGE OF HOSTILE DEATHS IN SOUTHEAST ASIA, 1964-1974

Service	Officer		Enlisted		Total	
Army	2.7	(3,393)	14.2	(27,470)	12.6	(30,863)
Marine Corps	.6	(785)	13.0	(12,274)	12.3	(13,059)
Air Force	1.1	(1,284)	8.1	(394)	2.9	(1,678)
Navy	.5	(384)	.3	(1,208)	.3	(1,593)
All Services	1.9	(5,847)	13.5	(41,346)	12.1	(47,193)

Total hostile deaths given in parentheses.
Source: recomputed from Department of Defense statistics.

The problems of the all-volunteer force are not to be found in the end of conscription, nor in the declining youth cohort of the 1980s, nor in the efforts of service recruiters. Rather, the grievous flaw has been a redefinition of military service in terms of the economic marketplace. There can be no question that this has led to a grossly unrepresentative enlisted force in the all-volunteer Army. The real question is how high-powered commissions and official studies can come up with an opposite conclusion.[10]

In the post-Vietnam context, if United States forces are to fulfill their function of military deterrence, representational concerns are still germane. This is not to argue that the composition of the enlisted ranks ought be perfectly calibrated to that of the larger society. It is not to raise the red herring of quotas, which are a moral affront as well as unconstitutional. However, it is to ask what kind of society makes it a matter of all but official policy to preclude its privileged from serving in the ranks of its Army. It seems a social reality that the combat arms will never draw proportionately from middle- and upper-class youth. But to foster policies that accentuate the tracking of lower-class and minority youth into such assignments is perverse. If participation of persons from minority or poor backgrounds in leadership positions is used as a measure of democratic character, it is even more important that participation of more advantaged groups in the Army's rank and file also be a measure of representational democracy.

Present and anticipated difficulties in recruiting an all-volunteer force have led to renewed talk of restoring conscription. This possibility is currently viewed as remote. However, a return to the draft would pose anew the question of who serves when most do not serve. Under present manpower needs, only about one in five males would be drafted or otherwise serve in the military. If women were to be drafted, the proportion of male youth serving would of course be only one in ten. A key factor that operated favorably during the peacetime draft of the 1950s was that because of the large size of the military and the small youth cohort (the maturing "Depression babies"), over three-quarters of the eligible men served in the military. This fostered a legitimization of the peacetime draft. In actuality, a higher proportion of men were drafted in the 1950s than during the Vietnam War.

To have a workable conscription requires also a national consensus of its need, especially within the relevant youth population. Such a consensus does not exist presently. For example, induction would likely lead to turbulence on many college campuses. Moreover, if compulsion is used, many will attempt to avoid military service, which will bring on other problems. Even under a seemingly "fair" lottery system, decisions would have to be made which will corrode the induction system. In any event, only a small and, by definition, unlucky minority would ever be called to serve. In a peacetime situation, we must make the all-volunteer force work rather than find ourselves embroiled in a debilitating draft controversy.

Granted conscription is not feasible, what about management steps that could be taken to improve manpower utilization within the all-volunteer framework? Here we run into the difficulty that almost all proposals in this vein—a kind of sub-optimal approach—do not address: the core issue of getting young qualified men into the combat arms and aboard warships. Neither lowering physical or mental standards for men nor increasing the number of women, neither greater reliance on civilian personnel nor more utilization of older military members, suit the imperatives of the combat arms. Large raises in military pay for lower enlisted personnel were the principal attraction to induce persons to join the all-volunteer force. This, however, has turned out to be a double-edged sword. Youth surveys show that cash motivates less qualified youth (for example, high school dropouts, those with poor grades) to join the armed services, while having a negligible effect on college-bound youth.

The central issue remains: is there a way without direct compulsion by which a cross-section of young men can be attracted into the combat arms and related tasks? Or to put it differently, is there a way we can obtain the analogue of the peacetime draftee in the all-volunteer era? I believe there is.

One step would be a two-year enlistment option (the term of a draftee) to be restricted to the combat arms, low-skill shipboard duty, aircraft security guards, and labor intensive jobs. The *quid pro quo* for such assignment would be post-service educational benefits modeled along the lines of the G.I. Bill of World War II. (Eligibility for the Vietnam-era G.I. Bill expired in 1976.) Because there would be no presumption of acquiring civilian skills in the military, the terms of such short service would be honest and unambiguous, thus alleviating a major source of post-entry discontent in the all-volunteer force.

To go a step further, the military could set up a two-track personnel system recognizing a distinction between a "citizen soldier" and a "career soldier." The career soldier would be assigned and compensated in the manner of the prevailing system, but with higher salary rates than at present. The citizen soldier would serve a two-year term with low active-duty pay and no entitlements, but with deferred compensation in the form of a G.I. Bill.

The immediate goal is to break the mind-set in the Department of Defense that sees the all-volunteer force in terms of econometric models. To regard the military as an occupation also raises nagging issues on the future of the armed services in U.S. society. The all-volunteer force as presently constituted has come to exclude enlisted participation by those who will be the nation's future leaders, whether in government, business, or the intellectual and academic communities. Rotating participation of middle-class youth would leaven the enlisted ranks and help reinvigorate the notion of military service as a widely shared citizen's duty.

The Congress must attend to governmental policies which undercut the all-volunteer force and the notion of citizen service. I refer to the $4.4 billion in 1980 given to college students in the form of federal grants and loans. We have created, in effect, a G.I. Bill without the G.I. It is surprising that no public figure has thought to tie such student aid to any service obligation on the part of the youths who benefit. It is philosophically defensible as well as downright practical to hold that any able-bodied young person who did not perform national service, whether civilian or military, should be ineligible for federal student aid.

Those who deny the salience of representational concerns, whether class or race, are bringing the American military to its knees. The overriding strategy should be to make governmental subsidies of youth programs consistent with the ideal that citizen obligation ought to become an essential part of growing up in this nation. The all-volunteer force, if it is to survive, must move in the direction of more social representativeness and be itself reflective of core and shared civic values.

NOTES

[1] Richard V. L. Cooper, *Military Manpower and the All-Volunteer Force* (Santa Monica, Calf.: Rand, 1977), pp. 209-16.

[2] U.S. Bureau of the Census, *Current Population Reports,* No. 333, p. 20.

[3] A. J. Martin, "Trends in DOD First-Term Attrition," in H. Wallace Sinaiko, ed., *First Term Enlisted Attrition,* Proceedings of a Conference held at Leesburg, Va. April 4-7, 1977, pp. 20-21.

[4] Les Aspin, *Sergeant York Isn't Welcome Anymore* (no publisher indicated, 1979), p. 8.

[5] Cooper, *Military Manpower,* p. 139.

[6] Harley L.S. Browning, Sally C. Lopreato, and Dudley L. Poston, Jr., "Income and Veteran Status," *American Sociological Review,* 38 (1973): 74-85; Sally C. Lopreato and Dudley L. Poston, Jr., "Differences in Earnings and Earnings Ability Between Black Veterans and Nonveterans in the United States," *Social Science Quarterly* 57 (1977): 750-66; and Roger D. Little and J. Eric Fredland, "Veteran Status, Earnings, and Race: Some Long Term Results," *Armed Forces and Society* 5 (1979): 244-60. See also the discussion in Charles C. Moskos, Jr., *The American Enlisted Man* (New York: Russell Sage, 1970), pp. 64-77.

[7] Bernard Beck, "The Military as a Welfare Institution," in Charles C. Moskos, Jr., ed., *Public Opinion and the Military Establishment* (Beverly Hills, Calif.: Sage, 1971), pp. 137-48.

[8] David R. Segal, Barbara Ann Lynch, and John D. Blair, "The Changing American Soldier: Work-Related Attitudes of U.S. Army Personnel in World War II and the 1970s," *American Journal of Sociology* 85 (1979): 95-108; Stephen D. Wesbrook, "Sociopolitical Alienation and Military Efficiency," *Armed Forces and Society* 6 (1980): 170-89.

[9] Gilbert Badillo and G. David Curry, "The Social Incidence of Vietnam Casualties: Social Class or Race," *Armed Forces and Society* 2 (1976): 397-406.

[10] For example, "There is no evidence to suggest that the armed forces are now or are in danger of becoming a 'poor man's Army'," Defense Manpower Commission, *Defense Manpower; The Keystone of National Security* (Washington, D.C.: Government Printing Office, 1976), p. 167. "The evidence presented here thus shows that the American military has not been nor is it becoming an army of the poor or the black." Cooper, *Military Manpower,* p. 231. "The quality of the active force is generally comparable with that of the draft era. . . . Concerns that the active force would not be representative of the society at large have not yet materialized." *America's Volunteers* (Washington, D.C.: Office of the Assistant Secretary of Defense, 1978): pp. 181-82.